FURTHER ADVANCE I
BENTON AND CONNI
CONVERT

Technology companies have amazing products—products with the potential to make a real difference to businesses and lives. But it can be hard for them to step 'above' the detail of the tech and explain exactly how it helps. *Connect, Convince, Convert* takes tech companies on a step-by-step process that will help them revolutionise their communication to their target market.

— Karl Sice
GM Arrow ECS, ANZ

There are two languages in business—product and value. Tech companies often speak product, but customers only understand value. In this book, Carol Benton provides the theory and tools that help tech companies learn to speak their customers' language. Invaluable.

— Angie Vaux
Founder, Women in Technology Forum

Can't recommend this enough. You'll learn the process that Carol took us through in our business. After working with Carol, our business was able to get to the heart of the value we offer our clients. The *Connect, Convince, Convert* approach has really helped us to communicate better with our audience and win more business. Do yourself a favour and read this book.

— Lawrence Pelletier
Sales & Marketing Director, Redcat

From 'What' to 'So What' is the concept at the heart of *Connect, Convince, Convert*. Technology companies have always been comfortable telling the world the 'What', or technological detail, of their product. But they struggle to articulate their 'So What', or their true value. In this book, Carol Benton gives real-world, practical advice on how to translate from 'What' to 'So What' and start communicating in a way that wins more business.

— Wayne Phillips
Former Industry Manager, IBM; Managing Director, Microsoft

The book *Connect Convince Convert* is both thought-provoking and stimulating in its approach to the vexed question of the communication of business 'value' to customers. Having spent over 30 years in the tech sector, Carol Benton understands the difficulty that tech companies face when attempting to communicate the true customer value of their offerings. In this book, she addresses the issue head on, with strategic and practical advice that will help any tech company to communicate in a way that brings in more business.

— **Bryan Ward**

Former Senior Consultant, IBM Consulting Group; Co-author of 'How to make a team work' in the Harvard Business Review

Carol Benton practices what she preaches in *Connect, Convince, Convert*. Her content is engaging, insightful, and practical. Tech companies will find it invaluable.

— **Andrew Upton**

Marketing Communications Manager, Toshiba Australia

If you're in a tech business and find yourself talking about products, not value, *Connect, Convince, Convert* will give you some great guidance on how to change your communication approach. Carol Benton clearly explains how to work out what to say, and how to say it, in a way that gets results.

— **Colin Page**

Former Sales Executive, IBM

We've used Carol's approach, and it works. With her help, we are confident that we have a really clear and meaningful message and that we speak directly to our key audiences.

— **Scott Munro**

Owner, FutureNet

I've seen first-hand the issue that Carol Benton addresses in this book— technology companies who have great products but struggle to get their message across to their target audience. *Connect, Convince, Convert* is a strategic approach and offers practical guidance. This is an essential read for anyone in the tech sector.

— **Marc de Marcillac**

Former VP Operations EMEA, Workiva

Connect, Convince, Convert is a must read for any tech company struggling to win and retain long-term, loyal clients. Carol Benton's combination of strategy and practicality make this the go-to for tech companies wanting to improve their comms and their sales wins.
— **Justin L.**
Executive Director at an IT Services Company

In *Connect, Convince, Convert*, Carol Benton addresses the dilemma faced by many tech companies—how do you talk value and not just products? She combines strategic thinking with practical advice and plenty of real-life examples, making this an essential book for any tech company wanting to step up their comms.
— **Jeff Kelisky**
CEO, Seedrs

As a business strategist, I repeatedly see companies that are great at what they do really struggle to articulate their value to their audience. This book is designed for them. Carol provides straightforward, easy-to-enact advice on creating a clear message that conveys to an audience the heart of what a business can really deliver.
— **Michele Carson**
Founder, Influence Business Strategy

The perfect book for any tech company wanting to 'speak their customers' language'. *Connect, Convince, Convert* offers the perfect mix of strategy and practicality, all in a clear, concise style.
— **Paula Da Silva**
Former EVP of Partners, Customers and Alliances (Global), CitiXSys

Carol Benton really gets the issues that face tech companies when they're trying to communicate. This book skilfully combines strategy with highly tactical advice.
— **Adem Sefa**
Strategic Customer Engagement Lead EMEA, Amazon Web Services

Loved this book! A much needed look at how technology companies can break through the communication barrier. Carol Benton's approach is easy to follow and highly practical.
— **Jane Dobson**
Senior Sales Director at a Large IT Multinational

A breath of fresh air! *Connect, Convince, Convert* tackles the age-old challenge of communication in an ever-changing world. In this book, Carol Benton provides a readily accessible framework that enables any company to communicate more effectively with their audience in their own language.

— Kerryll Prossor
Former Consultant & Delivery Executive, IBM

We've worked with Carol for many years, and her practical implementation of the strategies and tips in this book have helped us to communicate much more effectively with our target market.

— Josie Rae
Marketing Manager at an Electronic Access Technology Company

Communication is essential in any business, but for tech companies it is sometimes hard to switch from talking about products to talking about value. In this book, Carol Benton clearly sets out a strategy and guidelines for getting it right. Thoroughly practical and enjoyable.

— Andrew Brown
General Manager of Technology Sales, United Kingdom & Ireland, IBM

Connect, Convince, Convert is a great read for any tech company that wants to engage more effectively with their customers and prospects. We've used Carol's approach and it works!

— Rhys Warren
Founder and CEO, Sektor

To Saskia,

I do hope you enjoy
Connect, Convince, Convert

Carol Benton.

CONNECT
CONVINCE
CONVERT

How **tech companies**
can **win more business** using
the **power of words**

First Edition

Editing Services by Caitlin Freeman of Get Bookified
Book Cover, Typesetting and Layout Design Copyright © 2022 Maja Creative
Art Direction by Maja Wolnik of Maja Creative
Graphic Design by Monika Brzeczek of Maja Creative
Cover Photograph by Jesse Spezza of Transcend Media
Author Bio Photograph by Stephanie Hill of Total Capture Photography

ISBN PRINT: 978-1-7397668-0-1
ISBN EBOOK: 978-1-7397668-1-8

Published by Words2Win Books
www.words2win.global

CONTENTS

INTRODUCTION

Vos clients, est-ce-qu'ils vous entendent?
Est-ce-qu'ils vous comprennent?
Est-ce-qu'ils prennent de l'action?

No, please don't stop reading...it's in English from here.

But do think about what went through your brain when you read those opening words. I'd wager that many of you didn't understand what I said, and even if you did understand it, you probably felt confused as to why I was writing in French. If I carried on for much longer, I can guarantee that most of you wouldn't have wanted to continue reading.

Now, I invite you to ask yourself if it's possible that your audience ever feels the same way when you talk about your business. Do they feel confused? Do you use jargon they don't understand? Are you missing the mark with your communication because you're not speaking your customers' language?

I want to reassure you that if your audience doesn't understand you, it's not due to a lack of knowledge on your part—I knew exactly what I was writing in those sentences above, but that doesn't mean that you did.

Your missed communication is not due to a lack of passion, either—you could be fully committed to what you're saying, but that doesn't make it comprehensible to others.

Finally, it's not your audience's fault if they don't get your message. It's up to you, as the communicator, to use language they understand—just as it's my responsibility to write this book in your language. A lack of comprehension is no one's fault, but it does mean that you're missing out on opportunity.

The fact is that no one engages with something they don't understand.

I specialise in helping technology companies to harness the power of words to communicate with their audience. Using my process, companies learn to articulate the value they offer, which of course leads to winning more business.

Communication is at the heart of all business. It allows you to grow a great product or service into a thriving company, full of clients who want to buy what you offer.

Even the most compelling idea won't get very far unless you can communicate it effectively to others. The best innovation in the world can't thrive in a vacuum.

TECH BRAINS AND COMMUNICATION BRAINS

Technology companies are strong on creative ideas, products, and services, but they're not always adept at communicating effectively.

As an example, I worked with a company run by some super smart people who developed an Artificial Intelligence (AI) technology that understands customer buying patterns. Yet when it came to understanding their own customers, they struggled to 'speak their language'. Their communication was overwhelming in its technical jargon and detail, and it did not express how businesses could use their product. It was a clear example of the fact that a tech brain and a communication brain are two different entities, and that organisations need both to succeed.

That's where I step in. I specialise in helping technology companies to harness the power of words to communicate with their audience. Using my process, companies learn to articulate the value they offer, which of course leads to winning more business.

I utilise proprietary strategies, tools, and techniques to help my clients to develop a clear and consistent message, and I show them how to get it out to their market in written and verbal formats. The result for them is more customers—customers who rave about them, come back time and time again, and tell others how great they are.

Connect, Convince, Convert is the culmination of everything I've learnt from helping technology companies around the world to improve their business communication. Over the next ten chapters, I'll take you through those same strategies, tools, and techniques that I've used to help my clients succeed. You'll learn how to uncover the message at the heart of your business and get it out to the people who are ready and willing to hear it. You'll see practical examples of how to speak your audience's language in order to share your expertise and build credibility. You'll discover how to keep your clients and prospects engaged and lead them smoothly into closing the deal.

THE SEEDS OF CONNECT, CONVINCE, CONVERT

This book draws on my years of experience helping tech companies to solve the communication issues they face. Whilst the Connect, Convince, Convert process was born from my work with clients over the last decade, the seed was sown much earlier than that from my lifelong love of language and a thirty-year corporate tech career.

My love affair with communication started at the age of six, when I first learnt another language. From that early education, I discovered that there was more than one way to say something and be understood. I realised that if you and another person spoke a common tongue, you could forge a connection. From that moment on, language formed the backbone of my studies, right through to university.

I was then lucky enough to join one of the biggest and best tech companies in the world. How does a languages graduate come to work for a technology corporation, you might ask? A family friend who worked for IBM suggested I consider applying to the company.

'But I know nothing about technology. What would I have to offer?' I asked.

My friend replied, 'Carol, IBM wants people who can communicate. The technology is something they can teach you. But they need someone like you to facilitate the transmission of information. As a languages expert, you can help them do that.'

That was a conversation that changed my life. In July 1985, I started life as an 'IBMer'.

I received great technical training, but as I'd been advised, the primary skillset needed was my ability to 'translate'. I was able to listen to what the customer needed, to understand what IBM offered, and to build a communication bridge between the two.

My time at IBM included roles in technical sales, marketing, operations, and business management. I moved from the UK to Australia and back again—twice. I was the ANZ leader of IBM's point of sale division when it was acquired by Toshiba, and I had the interesting challenge of leading my team through the transition.

I loved the dynamism of the industry and the fact that I learnt (and still learn) something new every single day. I had a lot of fun at my job. I travelled, met some amazing people, and received a world-class business education.

In my time at IBM, I saw the very best of business communication, but I often saw the worst as well. I observed some masterful communicators, and I also saw many people struggle to express their message.

As a communication expert, I wanted to ensure that I could always articulate IBM's story to its best advantage and paint a clear picture that would engage clients. As I grew in my career, I worked out how to fix communication issues, watching and learning from colleagues, clients, partners, and distributors, and coming up with my own solutions to the problems they faced. Little did I know it at the time, but I was building the foundation for *Connect, Convince, Convert*.

> **I wrote this book because I realised that for all the organisations I have worked with directly, there are many others that face the same issues and could benefit from the Connect, Convince, Convert approach.**

So, when the time came to leave the corporate world, I decided to take my experiences and observations and use them to help people in the world of tech to communicate more effectively. It was again the words of someone else that propelled me to the next stage in my career. When I told my team at Toshiba that I was leaving, one of them said to me, 'Carol, what are we going to do without you? You're so good at writing proposals. You can pull all the ideas together and make them really clear and compelling.'

His comment was a lightbulb moment. I realised that my three decades of expertise had given me skills that were of real value. Shortly after that, I had a pivotal conversation with a former colleague, who now helped 'corporate escapees' to set up their own practices. Rather than looking for my next job, I decided to bring my knowledge to other tech businesses and help them as I had IBM and Toshiba. Six months later, Words2Win was born, and I began to share my insights with other technology companies.

I wrote this book because I realised that for all the organisations I have worked with directly, there are many others that face the same issues and could benefit from the Connect, Convince, Convert approach.

If you are a tech business that is struggling to communicate, this book is for you. I offer you my 'communication brain' to help you translate your technical excellence into meaningful customer language.

Within the pages of this book, you will learn practical strategies that will make your business communication more effective.

If you are a communicator in the tech industry, this book is for you too. The industry needs your skills, and the process I've developed will give you strategic insights for how to contribute to your company.

I thank you for choosing to read *Connect, Convince, Convert*. My aim is to provide you with new ideas, approaches, and techniques that will turn your prospects into loyal customers. You can read this book chapter by chapter, or you can use the workbook sections at the end of each chapter to transform this book into a practical program for your company. As a technology professional who understands the power of communication, you will benefit from the power of Connect, Convince, Convert to win more business.

1

Connect, Convince, Convert

TECHNOLOGY POWERS BUSINESS AND TRANS-FORMS LIVES.

In just about every field and facet of our lives, technology plays a role.

IT systems manage vast amounts of data to make business processes more efficient. Computers automate tasks with 100% accuracy, removing the potential mistakes that come from human error. Smart networks provide connectivity that allows us to do business anywhere in the world without having to leave our home or office.

AI systems take in information about their environment and build up the 'knowledge' to drive cars, understand human speech, and compete in strategic games. Technology in the classroom enhances learning and student outcomes. Advanced medical technology helps doctors and surgeons to provide ground-breaking treatments and life-saving interventions.

Automation guides and manages our transportation networks, enabling us to travel safely and move goods efficiently throughout the supply chain. In an increasingly precarious world, security systems stay vigilant 24/7, never tiring or missing a beat. Technology is with us as we shop, work, exercise, relax, transact, create, design, inform, and sell.

If you've picked up this book, the chances are that you are part of that world of technology. You are the instigators of innovation and development—you're good at what you do, and you help to bring the power of tech to the people who use it in their lives and businesses.

YOUR ROLE AND STRENGTHS

You may have many years of experience in the world of tech, and you've seen it develop and become ever more ingenious and pervasive over your lifetime.

Conversely, you may be relatively new to the industry, attracted by the excitement of a world where nothing stands still and there is always something new to learn and to contribute.

Maybe you design systems or code the software that drives them. Perhaps you put together different technologies to create business solutions. Maybe you sell technology or manage the people who do. You might be an entrepreneur, bringing your own innovative ideas to the market, or you might work for a technology company, large or small.

Whatever your role in the technology sector, you understand the power that technology has to enhance and transform. You get why it is so clever, and you realise the possibilities it unlocks. You know how to use it, get the best from it, and even how to fix it. You know your business—your piece of the technology puzzle—from the inside out.

YOUR GOALS AND ASPIRATIONS

Naturally, you want to share your knowledge and solutions with the world. You want to make a difference to people and organisations. You want to use your expertise to build a successful business, with clients who appreciate what your products or services can do for them. Whether those clients are multinational corporations or individual consumers, you believe your solution is something they cannot do without—you provide something that makes their lives easier, safer, more rewarding, more insightful, or more profitable. You want to be the 'must have' in your chosen market. You have developed your technology in order to make an impact on the world, and your goal is to see it do just that.

Maybe you want your clients to be as enthusiastic about your product or service as you are, so they can tell others and spread the word further. You want everyone to feel as strongly and passionately about your fantastic tech as you do.

Ultimately, you want to increase your sales and grow your business, allowing you to develop ever better solutions for your market.

In order to achieve that, you have to be able to communicate effectively with your target audience. It is essential that you communicate in a way that engages them and helps them to see what you can do for them.

THE CHALLENGE

There are many people in the technology sector who are great at designing, implementing, and talking technology; however, they often struggle to communicate effectively about the value that their tech offers. When a prospective client asks them, 'How exactly will your solution improve our business?' these companies may respond with a long list of technical specifications without ever explaining their business benefits in words that the prospect can understand.

Maybe you can identify yourself in this description. Maybe you find it easy to 'talk tech', but you struggle to articulate your business benefits to your audience. Having in-depth knowledge about a subject is not the same thing as being able to explain how it helps people.

Now, you may ask yourself, 'Why is that important? We're a technology company, and we're great at what we do. So what if people don't understand the value of our tech? We know it helps them, and that's all that matters, right? Where's the problem?'

It's important to convey your business benefits because technology doesn't exist in isolation.

Technology exists not for its own sake, but to solve a problem. Your tech makes things possible that were not possible before. It is there to make life or business easier, safer, more efficient, or more insightful for those who use it.

It's important because customers are only going to buy your technology if they understand what it can do for them.

Much as you might want them to, businesses don't buy technology because of its wonderful architecture or the design methodology behind it. They don't buy it for its speed, chipset, integrations, or any of the other host of clever features you've included. The users of your product or service don't select it for the tech itself, no matter how fantastic it is. They choose the solution that best offers an answer to their problem.

The only way your prospective customers will know if your solution is right for them is through the way you communicate your value.

It's important to convey your business benefits because technology doesn't exist in isolation.

You know your business and your tech inside out, and whilst that is great from an internal company standpoint, when it comes to engaging with the people who will buy and use your products, it's essential to see things from their point of view. In other words, you need to be able to see your business from the outside in.

Communication is the bridge between having a great product or solution and having a thriving business. If you cannot communicate your business benefits, you could well be losing prospective customers to a competitor with a clearer message.

So, if you want to share your technology with the world, ironically you need to see beyond your technology. You must communicate not just what it is, but how it benefits the people who use it.

THE TELL-TALE CLUES

You may not be sure if you are communicating as well as you could, so how can you check? What are some of the red flags that indicate that your messaging might not be as strong as your technology itself? Here are five clues that you may be losing business due to poor communication.

CLUE #1

You feel that your target audience simply doesn't 'get' what you do. They don't engage with your solution as well as you would want or expect them to. What you think is a clear message simply doesn't resonate with them.

WHATEVER YOUR ROLE IN THE TECHNOLOGY SECTOR, YOU UNDERSTAND THE POWER THAT TECHNOLOGY HAS TO ENHANCE AND TRANSFORM. YOU GET WHY IT IS SO CLEVER, AND YOU REALISE THE POSSIBILITIES IT UNLOCKS. YOU KNOW HOW TO USE IT, GET THE BEST FROM IT, AND EVEN HOW TO FIX IT. YOU KNOW YOUR BUSINESS—YOUR PIECE OF THE TECHNOLOGY PUZZLE—FROM THE INSIDE OUT.

CLUE #2

You're getting leads and interest, but not from the people you want to engage with. The people who end up contacting you are not your ideal clients—they're 'tyre-kickers', and they don't have a real need for what you do.

CLUE #3

You find it hard to maintain the connections you make. You have meetings, but then you struggle to get a follow up. You have people sign up for your newsletter, but then unsubscribe soon after. Your prospects visit your website, but they don't get much further than a short look at the home page.

CLUE #4

You're making great connections, but you're not able to convert them to sales. You feel forced into 'hard sell' tactics, or you find yourself lowering your prices or throwing in 'special offers' to get your prospects to buy. You may end up getting the sale, but you're left with reduced revenue and profits. You give away so many extras and discounts that the cost of winning the client becomes too high.

CLUE #5

You're making sales but not repeat sales. Clients buy once but don't come back again, and you get no referrals from your current clients. You may be getting people to buy from you, but these clients don't feel good about their decision afterwards because you've had to cajole them into a decision. Instead of feeling proud of their choice to do business with you, they feel pressured and coerced. Consequently, they don't return or refer you to others.

Any or all of these red flags are indicators that your communication is failing to connect with your customers. The solution to this problem is to engage the right audience with a clear message that articulates exactly how they will benefit from what you offer.

THE SOLUTION

Now, I want to reassure you that, as we touched on in the Introduction, your communication issues are not due to a lack of knowledge on your part. You're good at what you do, you have great products and services, and you know them inside out.

Nor is this disconnect due to a lack of passion or intent—no doubt you're driven and committed to providing a great solution.

It's also not due to a fault in your product—you have spent a lot of time, energy, and money researching and developing a quality offering.

Furthermore, there's no blame to be placed on your audience's shoulders—they're not doing anything wrong if they choose not to engage with your solution. After all, it's the responsibility of the communicator to speak in a way the audience can understand.

No, the source of the problem is this: You are not speaking to your customers in a way that clearly articulates the value that you bring to their business. Your words have not painted them a picture of how they will profit from your solution.

When you are immersed in the world of technology, it's easy to get used to its language. The language of technology becomes the 'norm'. It then becomes hard to 'translate' into words that have meaning for your audience. As a technology expert, you may well have had a STEM-based education and background. Whilst I don't want to fall into any easy clichés about STEM and communication, it is true that the way in which science, technology, and engineering disciplines traditionally communicate is not always best aligned with expressing a value message in an engaging, personalised way.

Customers are only going to buy your technology if they understand what it can do for them.

If you recognise yourself in the description above, I have two things to say to you:

Firstly, you are most definitely not alone. I have come across many excellent technical and business brains who struggle to communicate the benefits of their solution to their clients.

Secondly, you're in the right place. By reading this book, working through the exercises, and using the tips and templates, you will learn how to communicate more effectively about your technology. You'll start to see where you are doing things well and where you could improve your communication. The lessons in this book will help you whether you are creating your own content, driving a strategy for your team to create it, or briefing an external communication professional.

THE CONNECT, CONVINCE, CONVERT MODEL

So, what does this book cover? How do I propose to help you learn about effective communication in the world of technology?

→ We start by learning about the Connect, Convince, Convert process, which helps you communicate your business benefits to your clients at each stage of the customer journey.

→ We move on to the importance of having a strategy behind your communication. I will share a step-by-step guide for developing your strategy, ensuring that your message engages your audience.

→ After that, we will move into practical implementation. We'll learn about the ten ways in which tech companies communicate with their target audience. These include verbal and written formats, both corporate and individual. You'll learn how to map your current communications against these ten formats to see which you are doing well and which you could improve. This will help you build a clearly prioritised roadmap for enhancing your communication.

→ Next, we'll take a deep-dive into the Connect, Convince, Convert process, with a chapter dedicated to each stage, full of tips and techniques that you can apply immediately to your business.

→ The most challenging part of communication is often sitting in front of a blank screen, so I'll take you through practical structures and frameworks—one for each of the ten communication formats—to get you started. This will save you time, effort, and frustration.

→ Finally, we'll explore the outcomes of this approach to business communication. We'll look at several companies just like yours who have gained practical advantages from using the Connect, Convince, Convert process. This will show you the benefits that you, too, can realise by following the methodology I've outlined in this book.

The system I've developed shows you how to engage with the right people—that is, people who need and can benefit from the solution you offer. Your communication must hold up a mirror to them and their issues. When you do this, your customers will self-select in their engagement with you, giving you the assurance that you are talking to your target audience. Similarly, if you recognise yourself in the description above, you have identified yourself as the ideal reader for this book. If the strengths, goals, and hurdles I've outlined above match yours, then there will be plenty in this book to help you address them.

Please read on, and I hope you enjoy learning more about how to communicate effectively about your technology and the transformation it delivers.

2

What Does Connect, Convince, Convert Mean?

Effective communication is the foundation for winning more business. To be truly effective, communication must do three things — it must connect, it must convince, and it must convert.

But what exactly does Connect, Convince, Convert mean? Since it is the title of the book and the premise for the approach and methodologies that follow, it is worth taking a bit of time to explore this idea so that we're all starting from the same place.

CONNECT

Connect means finding the right audience and getting them to engage with you.

CONVINCE

Convince means making the audience believe that you can help them, and that you'll deliver.

CONVERT

Convert means getting your audience to take the next step on the journey towards doing business with you.

Not every single piece of communication will contain every one of these elements, but your overall message needs to include all three. If you do only one or two of these steps, you'll be missing a vital piece of the engagement puzzle.

Without connection, you are just another company out there talking about their product or service.

Without conviction, your audience is not going to trust that you can make a difference for them, and it's likely they won't progress any further with you.

Without conversion, they may trust you and understand what you have to offer, but they will have no reason or motivation to do anything about it.

NO ONE BUYS SOMETHING THAT THEY DON'T KNOW ABOUT, DON'T UNDERSTAND, OR DON'T BELIEVE WILL BENEFIT THEM.

CONNECT

You can think about connection as cutting through the noise of your competition. At any given moment, there are hundreds of companies competing for your audience's attention. There are over 1 billion websites in the world. Experts estimate that we are exposed to anywhere from 6,000 to 10,000 ads a day.

In fact, I remember reading a story about a marketing exec who decided to test this estimate of the number of ads we see in a day. The story goes that he gave up before he left the house to go to work. Why? He had already been exposed to so many ads by the time he'd listened to morning radio, skimmed the newspaper, opened his pantry to make breakfast, and logged on to check his email that he could say with confidence that 6,000 was a low estimate. He decided that he'd save the effort and stop counting.

If you google your own product or service, you're likely to find hundreds of thousands of sites. Just think about the emails, social media messages, and alerts you've received in the past twenty-four hours. We are bombarded with messages every waking hour; however, most of them won't make a connection.

Connection is being heard. When you connect, you find the people who are your target audience and give them a reason or desire to engage. You do this by speaking their language so that your voice cuts through the noise. Connection is the starting point for any communication. It is a piquing of interest, an 'I want to hear more'. Connection is a spark — a tiny burst of raw energy with massive potential.

This spark of connection is not yet alight, but it is something that could grow into a flame in time. With the right fuel, it can grow into something much bigger, warmer, and more powerful. When it is fanned and nurtured, it gets stronger. By contrast, if it is ignored and unfed, it can just as easily be extinguished. A spark is a beginning, full of possibility.

Connection is made (or lost) very quickly. For example, estimates of how long users look at your website before deciding whether to stay vary from 50 milliseconds to 10 seconds. Think of the final countdown for a spaceship launch. You have that amount of time to win your audience. Either the spark is ignited, or it's not.

A connection is forged in the moment that your audience sees there is something in it for them. They don't have to know all the details, but they feel that your offer is something they want to explore further. Their reaction is often personal, and for that reason it can be hard to predict. The spark could be a catchy title on an article. It could be a piece of content that includes the words they've been searching for. It could be face to face, visual, or verbal. A presentation, a video, or a meeting. Whatever the format, the message speaks to them and makes them want to hear more.

> **Connection is being heard. When you connect, you find the people who are your target audience and give them a reason or desire to engage.**

CONVINCE

Convincing your audience means showing them that you 'get' them and that you understand their issues and aspirations. It's about making them believe you can do what you say you'll do. You are good at what you do, and you can and will help them make a difference in their business. It is all about credentials and proof points. It's where you show them other customers you've helped so that they trust that you can do the same for them.

Whilst connect is often based on emotion — a gut feeling, an instinct, an interest — convince provides the evidence that strengthens your audience's connection to you. Conviction reinforces that initial bond and rewards your audience with concrete information. Convince is where you provide facts, statistics, and numbers.

If connection is a spark, conviction nurtures that spark and helps it grow into a flame. When you convince your audience about the strengths of your product or service, you build your connection into a relationship founded on trust. Unlike a spark, a flame has power and resilience. It gives warmth and light, and it is harder to extinguish.

CONVERT

When you convert your audience, you persuade them to take the next step on the journey towards becoming a client. If connection is the spark and conviction is the flame, then conversion is the roaring furnace. It is a source of power in which we forge new creation and growth.

Of course, the goal is to turn your target audience into paying clients. That aligns with the classic sales cycle, where 'convert' means the point at which the prospect signs the order. Although you have that goal in mind from the start, your audience may only be able to see as far as the next step. The key to achieving the convert element of communication is not to confuse your view of the world with that of your audience. One step at a time is far more effective than trying to get them to take a giant leap.

It is essential to remember that winning the deal is not a single-step process. Your audience may take many steps on their journey to doing business with you. The goal of communication that converts is to get your audience to take another step. If your audience loses interest at any step along the way, they won't reach the end of the journey with you. So, conversion is the process of persuading the audience to place their feet one after another until they reach the finish line. Eventually, this path will lead them to (fanfare please) the signing of the order, the exchange of cash. You will achieve the 'conversion' in the accepted sales meaning of winning the deal.

UNDERSTANDING THE CONVERSION PROCESS

Imagine that you are using stepping stones to cross a river. You haven't actually forded the river until you have taken the final step onto the opposite bank. There might be multiple paths across the water, some with more steps than others. The route each potential client takes and the time they take will vary, depending on their level of confidence. Some clients may be brave enough to take a big leap, whilst others may be more cautious and prefer smaller strides. Some don't mind getting their feet a bit wet along the way, and others assess every stone for balance and safety before they venture so much as a toe onto it.

The conversion process reminds me of a hike I did with my teenage son on the beautiful Wilson's Promontory in Australia. We came to a beach where we had to cross an inlet of fast flowing water. There were sandbanks, fallen branches, and a few stones for help. For me, these stepping stones felt too far apart, and I was not confident that I had enough strength and stability in my stride to make it across. Billy, however, had no such concerns. He leapt and bounded across like a gazelle whilst I took the long way round, walking inland to where the stream grew narrower and the boulders lay closer together. Billy crossed much faster than me, but he did have one slip, so he walked the next few kilometres with a wet left foot. I took a longer route, but my feet were comfortably dry for the rest of our hike. Neither of us took the 'right' way — there was no right way, just different options. However, we both got across to the other side in our own way and our own time, ready to enjoy the glorious scenery of the rest of the hike.

This experience of crossing the river illustrates a key element in the conversion journey. No matter the route that your potential client takes, you must ensure that they don't stop, give up, or turn back. In order to accomplish this, you may need to play the long game. Don't rush them into a situation where they feel so trapped

MOST COMPANIES DON'T JUST WANT TO GENERATE ONE-OFF CUSTOMERS; THEY WANT TO CREATE LOYAL ADVOCATES or uncomfortable that they refuse to place another foot on the path. Make sure that they can always see the next step and are eager to take it. Conversion is about keeping your client's eyes focussed on the end goal (the opposite bank) and making sure there is always a stepping stone under their feet when they are ready to move forward.

CONVERSION BEYOND THE FIRST SALE

In classic 'sales cycle' models, winning the deal is the final step, the end of the process. In reality, however, winning the first deal is actually just a step — albeit a very significant one — on a journey that ideally goes beyond that first purchase.

Most companies don't just want to generate one-off customers; they want to create loyal advocates.

When clients are loyal, they buy from you more than once, becoming repeat customers. I am sure you're familiar with the statistics that examine the cost effectiveness of increasing an existing customer's spend with you compared with the process of going out to find new customers. The generally accepted rule of thumb is that it costs seven times less to sell again to the same customer. In fact, the ratio will vary based on your industry, product, and the client themselves, but the general principle holds true.

Your audience may take many steps on their journey to doing business with you. The goal of communication that converts is to get your audience to take another step. If your audience loses interest at any step along the way, they won't reach the end of the journey with you. So, conversion is the process of persuading the audience to place their feet one after another until they reach the finish line.

When clients become advocates, they are so impressed with your product or service that they tell their network about you. Advocates are pure gold. They can explain what you do in language that resonates with their friends and colleagues. They generate warm referrals, which have a much higher closing rate than other leads. Having customer advocates is like having an extra sales team working for you.

In order to turn customers into loyal advocates, you must

understand that conversion doesn't stop the minute the prospect signs the metaphorical cheque.

As we will see in the coming chapters, effective communication is a cyclical process. Understanding this process allows you to create a spark, fan it into a flame, and grow it into a fire with which you can shape and forge new business. Armed with this knowledge, you're on your way to cutting through the noise, presenting yourself credibly, and guiding your audience over each stepping stone, allowing them to journey from prospect to client to loyal advocate.

NEXT STEPS

In the next chapter, we'll build on this knowledge of what Connect, Convince, Convert means. We'll explore one of the most common mistakes in effective communication. Businesses that focus their marketing on 'What' their product or service can do often fail to see the big picture. Clients don't care about 'What'; they care about 'So What.' In order to succeed, you must be prepared to answer the following question from a prospective client: 'I know what your business does, but what can it do for me?'

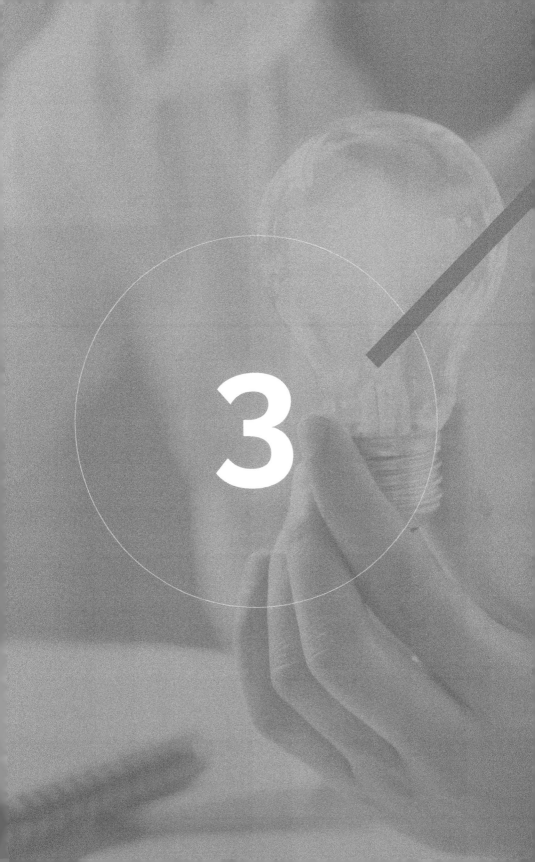

CHAPTER 3

From 'What' to 'So What'

Customers don't just materialise from nowhere. You create them. They exist as prospective clients, but you turn them into customers. Before that, they are individuals or businesses with an aspiration or a problem. Some businesses may be aware of the gap between where they are and where they want to reach. Others may not have even articulated this gap yet. Either way, they are looking for something — something that you can deliver. That's what makes them your target audience and your prospective clients. But what is the magic that turns them from frog to prince? How do they go from being a company that has never even heard of you to a customer who buys from you, returns to you, and sings your praises to others?

EFFECTIVE COMMUNICATION IS HOW.

Communication is the tool by which prospective customers find you and you find them. Communication helps you to draw them towards you, building and nurturing a relationship. Communication takes them on that journey from unknown prospect to loyal patron.

Think about it — there was a time when every one of your customers knew nothing about you, your company, or your product or service. Through communication they became aware of you, considered engaging with you, and finally decided to do business with you.

By the time they arrive at your metaphorical doorstep, a typical customer has been on quite a remarkable journey, from literally not knowing you exist to becoming a paying client and loyal advocate.

Every company wants to be able to take their prospects on that journey. If you asked 100 business owners if they wanted to turn prospects into profitable, happy customers, you wouldn't find a single one of them that would say no. Turning down that opportunity would be like saying no to turning base metal into gold. Who wouldn't want to enjoy the rewards of such an incredible transformation?

Effective communication — that is, communication that connects, convinces, and converts — is the vehicle that takes customers on that journey.

The concept of the customer journey is not new. The steps in the journey are known by a variety of names. One of the best known, for example, is Awareness, Interest, Desire, Action. If you take a moment to consider those words, you will notice that they are all nouns. They describe the customer's state. By contrast, Connect, Convince, and Convert are all verbs. The focus here is on something that you do. When you understand the customer journey in terms of verbs instead of a set of passive states, you realise that the onus is firmly on you to take action. It is your job to move the customer along the path towards you.

The more traditional customer journey models are not only passive; they also tend to be linear and stop once you get to action. The beauty of the Connect, Convince, Convert approach is that, as we saw in Chapter 2, 'Convince' simply means to get them to the next step. Yes, at some point, that next step will be a purchase. Then there will be another step, when they buy from you again, and another when they recommend you to someone else. So long as you keep taking action to convince, even once your prospect has become a client, this approach to communication is the gift that keeps on giving.

Now, as you know, there is an awful lot of communication out there — from websites to ads to messages — and much of it is ineffective. It fails to take the client on the journey from prospect to paying customer or loyal advocate. So, how do you entice your prospects onto that path and ensure they stay on track until the end?

THE ANSWER? YOU TRANSFORM YOUR COMMUNICATION FROM 'WHAT' TO 'SO WHAT'.

'WHAT' VS. 'SO WHAT'

As a technology business, you're probably very good at communicating your 'What'. Businesses across a range of sectors find this part of communication relatively straightforward. Your 'What' is your product or service. It's the nuts and bolts of what you offer. It's the technology, the delivery, the features, the 'feeds and speeds'.

Companies love to communicate their 'What'. They know it inside out; they live and breathe it. Their 'What' is their comfort zone. It doesn't require too much thought, so it's easy to talk about.

Unsurprisingly, many technology businesses focus their communication on themselves and their product specifications — their 'What'. Go to a website or pick up a brochure from any tech company, and there's a good chance that the first thing you'll see will be a 'What' message. I know of one large manufacturer, for example, that opens their website with the words, 'Exceptional Tech'. Another has the name of their chip in the second line. You may have even fallen into this same trap.

There's nothing wrong with explaining your 'What'. After all, your product or service is the heart of your business — it's what you sell and what generates your revenue. You have tech that you have developed and have invested in. You are proud of your product or service, and you know it does a great job. Of course you want to shout about it from the rooftops.

Your customers do need to know about the features of your offer — at the right time. As you will see, your 'What' makes up an essential part of the 'Convince' phase of effective communication. However, it is not the very first thing that your prospective clients need to know. During the initial 'Connect' phase, it is important to focus on building a relationship with your prospects. No matter how amazing your technology may be, endlessly bombarding your audience with facts about your products will not entice them to take this all-important journey with you.

THE POWER OF 'SO WHAT'

Now, you might reasonably ask, what are you supposed to focus on if not the nuts and bolts of your 'What'? Let me explain. When your prospective customer is reading your website or brochure, they are asking themselves one question: 'So What?' Your prospect primarily wants to know if your product or service can solve their problem. They are less interested in what you do than in what you can do for them. In order to connect with your prospect, you need to be able to answer them when they ask, 'So What?'

Your 'So What' is your value. It's what your product or service accomplishes for your prospective client. It is how you will change their business, their life, and their bottom line. It has meaning for them. It communicates how things will be different for them if they choose to work with you. You know 'What' you do, in the sense of the product that you offer, but 'So What' is about understanding that your clients want to buy a solution.

I want to acknowledge that it can be challenging to communicate a 'So What' to your prospective customers. 'What' is easy because you know your product inside out. 'So What' often feels uncomfortable because it involves seeing things not from the inside out, but from the outside in. It means stepping outside of your normal point of view, your comfort zone, and perceiving your business through the eyes of your prospective clients.

'So What' means understanding your prospects' aspirations and underlying needs. It involves expressing exactly how you can help them achieve their goals. It means making a radical shift in your thinking and realising that technology in itself is not the end game. Technology is only of value if it helps somebody attain or accomplish something.

If you want to know what 'So What' looks like, think back to October 2001, when Steve Jobs announced the iPod.

What he didn't say was that Apple was launching a portable media player and multi-purpose pocket computer, with an ARM processor, 512 MB – 256 GB of flash memory, and a cirrus logic audio codec chip.

Not that all of that isn't true or important, particularly to the smart people at Apple who developed it. However, that description is the 'What', and it almost certainly wouldn't have meant much to the audience that Jobs was targeting.

So instead, he used what to my mind is one of the best examples of a 'So What' statement ever created. Steve Jobs told the world that Apple was giving people '1000 songs in your pocket'.

It's simple, it's concise, and above all, it clearly articulates the issue that Apple was solving and the benefits that users would experience.

That brief little phrase, '1000 songs in your pocket', was shorthand for, 'You love to listen to music and would love having your music library with you everywhere you go. But it's just not practical to carry around a massive ghetto blaster and a heap of CDs. So, here is the solution to your problem'.

COMMUNICATING YOUR 'SO WHAT'

'So What' involves a 'translation' from speaking about 'What we do' to 'How we add value'. Jobs brilliantly translated the description of the smart tech that Apple had developed (what they do) into a message that illustrated how iPod users could listen to all their music anywhere, anytime (the value).

Making that translation can be as big a challenge for some as learning a new language. That said, when you do learn to articulate your 'So What', it has a massive impact on your ability to communicate with your customers. Remember the last time you heard someone speaking a foreign tongue that you didn't understand — you might have listened for a moment, but then you quickly lost interest. Or imagine watching a foreign language film with no subtitles — you probably wouldn't follow along for very long. However, as soon as there is a translator or sub-titles on the screen, everything becomes clear. Suddenly, there is meaning in the words that you are hearing, and you can engage in ways that you couldn't before.

That's the difference between you throwing technical jargon at your audience and showing them how your product is going to remove the obstacles from their path.

Moving from 'What' to 'So What' is the process of translating your jargon into words that will resonate with your customers. Like all foreign languages, 'So What' can take some time to learn, and translating is not easy. But if you are to be understood, it is essential.

The power of 'So What' comes from one very simple fact:

PEOPLE DON'T BUY PRODUCTS OR SERVICES; THEY BUY VALUE.

If you're of the more mathematical persuasion, you could think of it as an equation:

$$\text{'WHAT'} < \text{'SO WHAT'} = \text{VALUE}$$

Nobody buys something they don't comprehend, but remember, it's not the details of your technology that your customers need to understand — they need to grasp what your technology does for them.

For example, I know nothing about the workings of a car. I don't understand how the engine works, how the energy in the fuel is converted into forward motion, or how the complex circuitry manages and monitors all the components.

What I do understand are the benefits that a car has to offer, as well as the specific benefits of the car that I chose to purchase. I understand my car's fuel economy, safety, and comfort. These benefits made me choose my specific make and model of car over the other vehicles that were competing within the same market.

In fact, if you look at car manufacturers, they are a great example of an industry that sells value quite well. Whether that value is status, speed, space in the boot, fuel economy — the list goes on — the auto industry understands the needs of their different prospects, and they communicate their value based on those **By the time they arrive at your metaphorical doorstep, a typical customer has been on quite a remarkable journey, from literally not knowing you exist to becoming a paying client and loyal advocate.** needs. How many car ads have you seen that show the inner workings of an engine? None, I'll bet. Yet showing detailed engine schematics is the metaphorical equivalent of what so many tech companies still do.

GOING BEYOND YOUR 'WHAT'

At any given moment, you and your next potential client are circling each other in a kind of dance. Your prospective customer wants a solution to their problem, and they are willing to pay for it. You know that your product or service is just the thing they need to resolve their issue, and you want to make the sale. Effective communication is the alchemy that brings you into sync with your prospective client and allows you to close the deal.

Now, you might be thinking to yourself, 'I know that I have been communicating with a "What" message rather than a "So What" message, but I have customers, so something must be working'. Yes, it's true — some customers will find you on their own and decide to buy from you via your 'What' message. They have done their own research, they know exactly what they are looking for, and they are aware of the benefits your offer will bring. For these customers, a 'What' message will do the trick.

However, what about all the prospective clients who haven't done detailed research, and who can't 'connect the dots' themselves to understand what your solution will do for them? If your communication doesn't take this audience into consideration, you are missing out on a great deal of opportunity. You will lose the majority of your prospective clients if you don't answer their 'So What'. It is up to you to articulate the value of your offer in words that your prospect will understand.

We must also take into consideration the changing landscape of sales. Nowadays, you are far more likely to make first contact with a prospective customer digitally than face-to-face. These customers will come across your business via a marketing campaign, your LinkedIn page, or your website. Your competitors use the same platforms and marketing techniques, and they probably sit right above or below you on the same search engine results page. If they articulate their 'So What' more clearly than you, visitors won't spend long on your communication.

As you have seen throughout this chapter, your ability to close the deal often comes down to the fluency with which you speak your client's language in your marketing material. When you meet with a potential client in person, it is easier to identify the parts of your pitch that resonate with them. Being able to respond to them in real time allows you to adapt your pitch to their specific needs. When you are communicating via a one-way digital medium, however, you must anticipate your prospect's questions, objections, and desires in order to communicate the value of your offer. If you hit them with a litany of technical specifications, you will lose them to your competition.

TRANSFORMING 'WHAT' INTO 'SO WHAT'

BACKGROUND

I worked with a client whose core business is IT support and rollouts. Their message, articulated in a capability statement, focused on the skills of their people, the breadth of their infrastructure, and the flexibility of their engagement models. They highlighted their project management capabilities, the sheer number of projects they had run, and the effectiveness of their helpdesk. All of these statements were true; however, none of this language explained the value that the company offered their clients.

They engaged me to help them develop the content for a new website, and we dug into just what their value really was (using the process that we'll discuss in the next chapter). They discovered that when they applied the 'So What' principle, their value became clear — they offered their clients consistent outcomes, the ability to plan implementations that did not impact business operations, and ultimately a faster rollout. The whole reason their clients implement new technology is to derive business benefits, so a smooth and rapid rollout means that they get to achieve those business benefits sooner. That's the real 'So What' of my client's service.

SOLUTION

The company decided that the features they had highlighted in the capability statement were still relevant, so we listed them on the lower-level pages of their website. When prospective clients now go to the company's homepage, they feel represented and understood. The very first message that they see acknowledges their struggles, recognises their needs, and paints a picture of the business benefits they will gain from the company's offer.

Translating 'What' to 'So What'

1. What are some examples of 'What' that you have written in your business' marketing language?

2. What do your customers value most about what you have to offer? How does your product or service solve their problems?

3. Now write some 'So What' descriptions that articulate the value that you add to your customers' lives.

4. Observe the differences between your old 'What' statements and your new 'So What' descriptions.

Clarifying Your 'So What'

If you're not sure how to get from 'What' to 'So What', here is an exercise that will help. I have adapted this from the 'Five Whys' technique, which is an approach used to find the root cause of a problem by asking 'Why' five times, with each answer becoming the starting point for the next question.

In this version, we replace 'Why' with 'So What' — i.e. 'What does your offer enable the client to do?' You ask the question until you drill down to a genuine business benefit.

Business benefits usually fall into one of five broad categories, which can be summarised as follows:

→ Make more money
→ Save money
→ Develop a new product or service
→ Make customers happier
→ Avoid risk/be compliant

In this exercise, you enter a statement from your current messaging and ask, 'So What?' You may not need to go through five iterations — you can stop when you've reached a business benefit.

In the example below, I've shown how this model could apply to the client I described in the case study above, helping them to think about the benefits for their customers. At the end of the chapter, there is a blank worksheet for you to use to clarify your client's 'So What'.

FEATURE

We have 100 engineers around the country.

SO WHAT?

FEATURE

That means we can roll out to more sites in parallel.

SO WHAT?

FEATURE

That means our clients can achieve their new technology implementation faster, as they're not waiting for engineers.

SO WHAT?

FEATURE

That means their new systems will go live sooner.

SO WHAT?

FEATURE

That means they get the benefit of their new systems — cost savings — faster.

SO WHAT?

THE CLIENT'S BUSINESS BENEFIT

Our offer enables our client to save money.

YOUR FEATURE

SO WHAT?

YOUR FEATURE

SO WHAT?

YOUR FEATURE

SO WHAT?

YOUR FEATURE

SO WHAT?

YOUR FEATURE

SO WHAT?

YOUR CLIENT'S BUSINESS BENEFIT

NEXT STEPS

In the next chapter, we'll look at how we can position our-selves in order to express value. This involves a strategic approach, one that answers five essential questions that uncover our true value in our clients' terms. We'll look at the benefits of taking a strategic approach so that we're not trying to reinvent a value statement every time we communicate. Once we define our value message, we will be able to express it clearly, consistently, and with 100% customer focus.

4

The 5 Steps to Building a Message Strategy

LET'S RECAP

We have explored the three elements of effective communication and what each one means. We've explained how communication takes prospective clients on the journey to becoming loyal customers and advocates of your business. We've experienced the power of 'So What' over 'What' in propelling prospects along that path. All of these points are good in theory, but if we're to use this knowledge, we need more than theory. We need to understand how to put these strategies into practice.

EXPLORING YOUR 'SO WHAT'

In order to delve into your 'So What', you need to answer five key questions. These questions will help you to see your business from all angles, including looking 'from the outside in'. This process will ensure that you consider your prospective client's point of view as well as your own internal priorities.

The answers to these questions will allow you to create a message strategy. A message strategy is a documented plan for how you are going to communicate, ensuring that your message meets the triple requirement to connect, convince, and convert. A message strategy is the 'master source file' — it means you don't have to reinvent the wheel each time you communicate, ensuring that your message remains consistent, clear, and customer-focussed.

THE IMPORTANCE OF STRATEGY

You have a strategy for other areas within your business — for example, you plan your product development approach, your financial management, and your growth, whether that is organic or via acquisition. Successful businesses understand the need for a strategic view of the world.

It is no different with your message. Without a clear strategy, your marketing efforts become mixed and confused — you express one idea through one medium this week, and another idea through a different medium the following week. This wastes valuable resources because your prospective clients won't be able to discern a clear message that they can act on. Taking a strategic approach involves some planning up front, but the benefits outweigh the effort.

CONSISTENCY

A message strategy underpins all business communication. It clarifies your thought process, ensuring that when you communicate, you do so in a way that is consistent. Consistency has two aspects to it — time and format. Your message needs to remain consistent from day to day, week to week, month to month. It also needs to be consistent over different media, meaning that what prospective clients see on your website, for example, should be the same message they get when they meet your team, browse your LinkedIn profile, or read your blogs and eBooks.

That's not to say that communication about individual products won't change, or that your message won't evolve over time; however, the fundamentals will ideally remain consistent. The most successful message strategies tend to be long term ones, telling the market what you offer and what you stand for. Consistency is an element of understanding and credibility.

It is tempting to think that you need to refresh your messaging — this is because of the disconnect between the transmitter and the receiver of information. We tend to think that as soon as we've said something once, we have communicated. We may even believe that having a consistent, unchanging message will bore our audience. The reality is that the person receiving the information may have to hear it multiple times before it is truly received and understood.

'The single biggest problem in communication is the illusion that it has taken place' — George Bernard Shaw's pithy quote applies to modern day communication just as much as it did in the first half of the 20th century.

There are numerous examples of successful businesses that have taken this approach with their key messaging — including Nike, who have been using 'Just Do It' as their message since 1988.

Not surprisingly, the number of times that someone has to hear your message before it is understood, remembered, and acted upon is an inexact science. It depends on many factors, including the complexity of the message, how well the message resonates with the listener, and the number of competing messages. Received wisdom puts the actual number anywhere between three times and twenty times, with the 'rule of seven' being popular amongst marketing experts.

The key takeaway, though, is that whatever the number, your message won't be consistent unless it is strategically planned.

Without a strategy, we risk wasting our time and communication budget on 'scattergun' content that is not consistent, not well thought out, and not targeted to a specific audience. This type of content is far less likely to connect, convince, and convert; in fact, it has a high probability of confusing our audience.

THE FIVE QUESTIONS

Creating a message strategy starts by answering five key questions. Let's take a look at why each of these questions is important for developing a message that connects, convinces, and converts.

The five questions are:
1. Why do you do what you do?
2. Who is your target audience and what are their issues, goals, and aspirations?
3. What do you offer to help your audience achieve their goals and/or address their issues?
4. What makes you good at what you do and sets you apart from others?
5. How will your audience benefit from working with you?

QUESTION 1: WHY DO YOU DO WHAT YOU DO?

It's easy to assume that when we make business decisions, we do so on a rational basis, relying strongly on facts and evidence, not emotion. In fact, I suggest that the majority of us would say that we use logic when it comes to business. However, studies show that the brain's decision-making process is not quite that clear-cut. Emotion plays a bigger part in our decisions than we may realise.

As we will see, we make our decisions based on emotion, and then we use facts to rationalise that decision afterwards. For this reason, the very first question to answer is one that uncovers the passion that underpins your business. You need to communicate your 'why' in order to make the emotional connection that is part of all business decisions.

Post-Hoc Rationalisation

The discovery of the role of emotion in decision-making was made by Professor Raj Raghunathan and Ph.D. student Szu-Chi Huang at the McCombs School of Business at the University of Texas.[1] The research team at McCombs were interested in how people make decisions — whether more weight was really given to logic, or whether feelings

---

[1] Simon, Jeremy M., editor, *Do You Make Buying Decisions Based on Logic or Emotion? A Tale of Two Chickens*, McCombs Today, The University of Texas at Austin, April 2010, mccombstoday.org/2010-04-do-you-make-buying-decisions-based-on-logic-or-emotion-a-tale-of-two-chickens/.

The single biggest problem in communication is the illusion that it has taken place. — George Bernard Shaw.

play a larger part than previously imagined. Their work showed that emotion and facts are equally important when it comes to the brain's decision-making process. Both play a part, but at different stages. Decisions are made on emotional response and then, once made, are rationalised based on fact.

They discovered this using, of all things, pictures of chickens.

The researchers showed participants photos of two different chickens — one was plump, white, and covered in feathers. It looked like the perfect image of a chicken from a children's picture book.

The other chicken was bald, skinny, pink, and had stunted wings — very unattractive.

All participants were given several facts about these chickens. The first piece of information given to them was that the plump chicken was natural and the skinny chicken was genetically engineered.

Unbeknown to the participants, however, they had been divided into two groups, and the second piece of information they were given differed by group.

→ Group A was told that natural chickens are healthy but less tasty, and genetically engineered chickens are tasty but less healthy.

→ Group B was told the opposite, that natural chickens are tasty but less healthy, and genetically engineered chickens are healthy but less tasty.

NATURAL
CHICKEN

GENETICALLY
ENGINEERED

A. Healthy, less tasty
B. Tasty, less healthy

A. Tasty, less healthy
B. Healthy, less tasty

The participants were then asked to select their preferred chicken. Regardless of the group they were in, all the participants selected the plump, white chicken.

Here's where the experiment gets really interesting — when the participants were asked why they had made their choice, those in Group A said it was because they felt that health was the most important factor, whilst those in Group B said they valued taste above all. No one openly justified their choice based on how they felt about the chicken's looks. Rather, they rationalised their emotional choices with non-emotional reasons, to the point that the two groups found completely opposite ways to justify the same decision.

A second experiment asked participants to evaluate the work styles of opposing political candidates. Participants were asked to rate the effectiveness of the approaches displayed by two politicians, a Republican and a Democrat.

The participants were again divided into two groups. The first group was told that the Republican used work style A and that the Democrat used work style B. The second group received the opposite information. Participants were then asked which work style they felt was more effective.

Regardless of the work style, participants made their decision in line with their political leanings. The participants who were Republican preferred the work style they believed was shown by 'their' candidate, and the same was true for the Democrats.

The research team at McCombs called this phenomenon 'post-hoc rationalisation', which is the fact that we make decisions based on emotion and then justify those decisions with logical criteria. The researchers believe this is because our society doesn't see emotion as justifiable grounds for a decision. We value logic and science more highly than emotion, so we use them to come up with the reasons behind our choice. This is an unconscious process but understanding it can help us to ensure that our message is heard.

Knowing about post-hoc rationalisation helps you to create a message that includes an emotional element — the 'why' behind your business. If you can share some of the passion that drives you, the reasons *why* you're in this game, you'll stand a stronger chance of making an emotional connection with your audience, which, as research shows, is very hard to dislodge.

Engaging with a business because of its 'why' is now more important than ever. In 2021, Forbes asked professionals from Forbes Agency Council for their insights into key marketing trends. One of the market shifts identified was towards 'meaning and purpose'. The Forbes report stated that, 'Knowing your "why" helps differentiate you from the competition and stand in an authentic place. That attracts customers. Coming from a place of purpose will drive marketing to new heights and bring customers better suited for what you have to offer'.[2]

When a business forms a strong bond with a client, it is based not only on what they do, but on who they are. If you want to create a relationship that is long-term, one where the customer engages with you again and again and refers you to others, it is not enough to simply solve a short-term problem. As we will see later in this chapter, you need to connect your offer to the customer's dreams and aspirations. One of the strongest ways to build this connection is to share your 'why'. Your client wants to feel that you are a friend who is on their side. If you can create an engaging customer experience — as Jobs did

[2] Golodner, Lynne, et al. '15 Top Marketing Trends To Keep An Eye On In 2021'. Forbes, Forbes, Inc., 27 January 2021, www.forbes.com/sites/forbesagencycouncil/2021/01/27/15-top-marketing-trends-to-keep-an-eye-on-in-2021/.

CAROL BENTON

brilliantly with Apple — you will develop relationships that are driven not just by short-term purchases, but by long-term loyalty.

QUESTION 2: WHO IS YOUR TARGET AUDIENCE?

The Cocktail Party Effect

Imagine this scenario — you are at a large party, surrounded by blaring music and the chatter of dozens of voices. The hubbub is so loud that you find it hard to hear even the conversation going on next to you. Yet, when someone across the room calls your name, it cuts through the background din, and you hear it as clear as a bell. Linguists have long recognised this phenomenon — the way that our brains can filter out 'meaningless' information yet focus on messages targeted specifically at us — and they have dubbed it 'the cocktail party effect'.

The cocktail party effect is a perfect example of a message being heard above the background noise. It illustrates one of the most important techniques that we can use to ensure that our message gets to the right ears, above all those competing voices. Using this technique, we can talk directly to our audience, metaphorically using their name. However, in order to successfully implement the cocktail party effect, we must first develop a detailed profile of our ideal client.

We make decisions based on emotion and then justify those decisions with logical criteria.

Communicating with Your Target Audience

The messages that we hear most clearly are those that we believe are intended for us to receive. We are programmed to differentiate between background chatter and communication that we deem to be important, like our own name. The same is true in business communication — we focus on the things that have the most meaning and relevance to us. So, it makes sense that when you want to express your message, you need to select a target audience that will respond positively to what you have to say, and you need to tailor your message to your audience's precise requirements. You're aiming for the audience who is the least likely to filter out your message and the most likely to hear it above the background racket.

When you plan your message strategy, you must narrow down your target audience to a specific demographic profile. If you find this process challenging, you are not alone — this is where many organisations struggle. We all have a natural tendency to assume that the more widely we spread our message, the more responses we'll get. We worry that if we target one section of the market, others won't buy. Although it may feel counterintuitive, the truth is that the more specific the message, the better the response. When you define your audience, you can tailor your message to their needs, and they will be more likely to hear you. It is the marketing equivalent of using their name in a crowded party.

On the flipside, if you try to be everything to everyone, your message will end up being too vague — no one will think you are talking directly to them, and therefore no one will listen.

In order to direct your communication towards a specific audience, you must first identify who they are. Then you can determine the goals they want to achieve and the hurdles that stand between them and success. Once you create a detailed profile, you can express your offer in a way that addresses their particular business needs.

Defining Your Target Audience

There are many characteristics that could define your target audience. If you are in a business to consumer (B2C) market, your criteria might include gender, age, location, attitude to technology, and disposable income.

In the business to business (B2B) world, one of the most commonly used definitions is industry. Industry can be useful for identifying goals and hurdles — there are often commonalities between companies within the same industry segment. However, industry isn't everything — there other factors to take into account when determining the profile of your target market.

CUSTOMER DEFINITION

You may have more than one type of ideal client, in which case you would define multiple groups and create a variant of your message for each. For example, I worked with a client whose business is distribution. They have two sets of target audience — the manufacturers whose equipment they distribute and the clients to whom they sell it. The aspirations and goals of each audience are different, and therefore my client had to create two messages. There was overlap between the two (particularly in their 'What'), but their 'So What' was different for each audience.

Another company I worked with sells their own product, but they distribute it indirectly via partners. They have one message for their end users and a different flavour of their message for partners.

Once you have categorised your target audience, you'll need to ensure you understand their goals and aspirations if you are to speak to them not only by name but also 'in their language'.

Issues, Goals, and Aspirations

When I went through basic corporate sales training, the mantra was 'start with the customer issue'. It is certainly true that unless the target customer has an issue, they will not need a solution. However, there's a bigger picture, one that includes the target audience's goals and aspirations, as well as their existing strengths and successes.

In the simplest sense, an issue is something that is stopping someone from reaching their goal. Whilst we certainly need to understand our audience's issues, we also need to look at the bigger picture — what are their aspirations and dreams? What do they ultimately want to achieve in the long term?

If you communicate about solving issues, your message will cut through the noise and resonate with your audience; however, there may be other companies trying to connect with your audience based on solving the same issues. Without going the extra mile, you risk your message getting lost in the crowd and becoming just another 'me too'. You may make a sale, but this transaction is less likely to be the start of a long-term, repeat business relationship. It's more likely to be a commodity sale, one where you are easily replaced if someone cheaper, faster, or better packaged comes along.

If, however, you can communicate in a way that taps into your target audience's higher level strategic goals, you can take your message to an altogether different level. This level of inquiry gets to the very heart of why your audience is in business and what they truly value. If you link your marketing to your audience's 'why', you have a powerful message indeed. This puts you into a much smaller competitive pool because the number of other businesses who can take this approach will be smaller than those who can provide a commodity product.

Finally, when you communicate with your target audience, it is also important to articulate their strengths. What have they already achieved, and what are they good at? Your audience will find it less appealing to engage with you if you focus solely on their shortcomings and issues. You can win them over by first recognising their capabilities and accomplishments.

Validation

It's all very well and good to sit down within your organisation and plan out what your target audience's goals may be. However, as we've seen, if you wish to communicate an effective message, you must see things 'from the outside in'. It's important, therefore, to validate any issues and goals that you presume your audience may have with data derived from outside your own organisation.

The best ways of doing this are:

1. Contacting your existing clients. The most direct source of information comes from your existing clients. Ask plenty of questions, take detailed notes, and learn from what they have told you about their business. Other techniques include asking these clients to participate in customer feedback surveys or be the subject of a case study.

2. Using your target audience's own communication. Read your prospective clients' websites, their annual reports, and the feedback they receive from their own customers. The information is all there — find it, check it, and test it with them to confirm that you are on the right track.

3. Researching industry data. Seek out analysts' reports and rankings (e.g. Gartner Magic Quadrant). Be aware of regulatory changes that may affect how businesses appear in these reports.

4. Searching social media. Look for posts, blogs, and articles that ask a question or request feedback on a key issue.

The goal of the validation process is to reach the point where you are crystal clear about who your target audience is (and isn't). When you can articulate what drives them, you can tailor your message to align with their goals.

Don't Boil the Ocean

It is important to stay focussed when developing your strategy. If you know your target audience well, you will almost certainly be able to identify aspirations and goals that fall outside the scope of your solution.

Whilst it may be interesting to understand these additional aspirations from the perspective of your message strategy, you are only looking to capture those goals where you can actually make a difference. If your message includes your client's broader aspirations, but it doesn't offer a clear path to achieve them, it will appear incomplete and less credible. These 'orphan' aspirations do not endear you to your audience. Although your prospects may appreciate that you understand their bigger goals, they will be disappointed that you cannot help them get there. In this way, don't 'boil the ocean' and try to capture every single one of your audience's aspirations in your strategy document.

QUESTION 3: WHAT DO YOU OFFER?

If you're used to creating 'What' messages, you'll probably assume that this is the easiest question to answer. This is the bit that you are already good at — it's the part of the message strategy that you know best. It's about you and your solution.

Not so fast. There are still a few traps to be aware of, and that can sometimes make this the hardest part to capture and communicate. Mainly because:

1. We know so much about what we offer that we risk bombarding our audience.
2. There is so much information that it can be hard to know where to start.
3. Different audience groups need different information, but we feel we have to tell everybody everything.

The solution lies in how you structure the information about your product or service so that it resonates with your target audience. There is a great deal that you could tell your audience about your solution — you know it inside out and in detail. The trick is not to try and say it all at once. You have to know what information to give your audience first, and how to gradually expand on it so that you build a convincing pitch. Connection sparks curiosity. Don't drown your audience with a tsunami of information; instead, give them a sip that encourages them to ask for more.

As part of this strategy, we need to capture all the key elements of the solution. Don't limit your solution description to the physical features — in fact, your real differentiation may lie in your pricing model, your delivery service, or your after sales support. When you begin to describe your solution, you will find that there are different levels of information that you need to communicate, depending on what stage the customer has reached in their journey towards you.

The next step in this process is to organise the information about your product or service into a hierarchy, or pyramid.

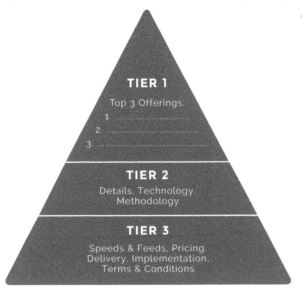

At the very top is a summary of what you offer, in three categories. 'But', you say, 'we offer far more than three products!' Or perhaps you say, 'We have a whole range of services! We can't list only three!' Yes, but *what you offer* and *how you communicate what you offer* are two different things.

We start with a triad because the 'rule of three' reflects the fact that words or ideas grouped into threes appeal to the pattern-seeking nature of our brains. Most people can remember a group of three things — it doesn't overwhelm us, and it is simple to comprehend. No matter how broad your range of offerings or how many different products you have, there will be a way to group them (at least at the highest level) into three categories.

This grouping may consist of the three things that you help your clients achieve, or it may be the three broad categories of your products, but believe me, it is possible to create this top-level hierarchy. It may take some time, but it is worth the effort to get it right because it will have a massive impact on the clarity of your message. As you start to turn your strategy into real-world forms of business communication (which we'll cover in detail in the next chapter), you'll find that a group of three is the perfect place to start your communication, especially in the 'Connect' stage.

Here are some examples of using the 'rule of three' as part of your overall marketing strategy:

→ Organising your elevator pitch into a three-point structure makes it easier to convey during a busy networking event.

→ Grouping your top three solutions on your website's homepage creates an orderly and visually pleasing design.

→ Focusing on the three main features of your business keeps your audience engaged during a presentation.

Your communication needs to start with this high-level information if you want to make an emotional connection. Even if you are operating in the B2B world, your target audience is still made up of individual human beings who cannot turn off or alter the way their brains make decisions. If you miss out on making this crucial emotion-based step, it becomes nigh on impossible to get to the next step in the process.

TIER 2

If your audience has engaged with your easy-to-process trio of products or services and they want to know more, you have the opportunity to convey more detail about your solution. This is where you reach the second tier of the pyramid. Remember, you're not drowning them in details; you just have additional information for them if and when they want it.

For example, you might wish to communicate more specifics on what each product or service achieves, or maybe you want to delve into the technology that it's based on. (Finally, you get to talk about your tech!) You could describe your methodology or the different modules within your software offering.

This information is particularly important for the 'Convince' stage of effective communication when your prospect has 'chosen their chicken', so to speak. They have made an emotional connection with you, but they need facts and details for their 'post-hoc rationalisation'.

So, think about what your Tier 2 information is going to be — what does your audience need to know at this second stage? Now that you have caught their attention, you need to give them something worth listening to.

Finally, we arrive at the base of the pyramid, or Tier 3. This is where you get the opportunity to provide even more detail to those members of your audience who want or need it. This is typically required once you are moving into the 'Convert' stage of effective communication. This information could include the nitty-gritty of your technical specifications and your 'feeds and speeds'. It could also include the practical details of purchasing from you, including pricing, delivery, and terms.

No single tier is more important than the others. They are all needed, but they have to be organised and grouped so they can be presented to your audience in the right order.

Prospective clients don't work their way up the pyramid from the bottom. If you flood your prospects with information and miss the first vital step of giving a clear and concise summary, you'll lose them to a competitor with a better understanding of the sales process.

Once your prospects have got through Tier 1 and have started to engage, it's important to have factual information ready for them to consume. Just as your audience may find it overwhelming to have too much data when they first discover you, they'll also be frustrated if they want to learn more, but your information isn't readily available. A drought is as dangerous as a flood.

By the time someone gets down to reading Tier 2, they are on the way to being convinced, or 'bought in'. The details that you provide in Tier 3 carry your prospects on the final part of the journey, allowing them to sell your idea to themselves. Alternatively, they may need to build a business case to present to someone else in their company. It's common for one person to be tasked with research and asked to make a recommendation to the higher-ups within their company. The person making the recommendation is not necessarily the person signing the proverbial cheque. In a scenario where you are relying on a recommender to make the case for buying from you, your Tier 2 and Tier 3 information has to be clear and easy to understand because it is going through a third party rather than coming directly from you.

You could also think of the three tiers in terms of a website structure. Tier 1 is the home page, with a clear and simple message. Tier 2 comprises the three separate, dedicated solution pages, which visitors reach by clicking through from the home page. Tier 3 is like the downloadable PDF that your prospects access from the solution pages, which includes spec sheets or an eBook.

Within our model from Chapter 2, Tier 1 is what drives connection, Tier 2 conviction, and Tier 3 conversion. Since we use different forms of communication to connect, convince, and convert, the information that we use in the different tiers naturally conforms to the respective format. We'll explore this more in Chapter 5.

One final thought about offerings. At this point, you may know your solutions better than you know your customers' problems. So, after considering this question of what you offer, it can be a good idea to go back round the problem/solution loop. There may be a feature of your solution that sets you apart from your competition for which you haven't yet identified a client problem.

QUESTION 4: WHAT ARE YOUR CREDENTIALS AND DIFFERENTIATORS?

Your ability to express your value ensures that your prospective clients will pick you rather than your competition. It is therefore important to articulate what you are good at and what sets you apart.

Think of it this way: if someone asked you, 'Give me the three reasons why we should do business with you', do you have the answer ready to go? I find it amazing how many business owners, salespeople, and executives stumble over what should ideally be on the tip of their tongues. So, do you know what makes you different, and can you clearly articulate your 'three good reasons'? These 'three good reasons' are based on your credentials and differentiators.

Credentials

Credentials are the proof points that back up our statements about being good at what we do. They may be formal qualifications, skills, or expertise. They may also be external awards or certifications.

Imagine if a potential client asked you, 'How do I know that you can actually do what you're telling me you can do?' The answer would be based on your credentials. One of the most powerful credentials is the words of other people. Your audience will expect you to say that you're good at what you do, but if someone else says it, their words carry more weight than yours.

A word about awards — I am sure that, like me, you have seen the words 'award-winning' countless times in business communication. You may have even used this kind of language in your own marketing. Awards can be a strong credential, but it is important to put some context around them when you present them as such. For a start, not all awards are created equal. Some are genuine industry accolades,

BUSINESS BENEFITS ARE IN THE 'EYE OF THE BEHOLDER'. A BENEFIT FOR ONE PROSPECTIVE CLIENT MAY NOT BE A BENEFIT FOR ANOTHER awarded by a panel of knowledgeable judges or by customer votes, for example, and they really do reflect excellence. Others hold less value. The key question is always, 'What does the award say about you and your company?' What is the context in which you won it? Does the context support your marketing communication? There is nothing wrong with using an award as a credential, but it is important to explain what it says about you and your business.

The same is true for statements attesting that 'we are number one'. When I worked for a corporate IT company, we were number one for market share in our industry by a large margin. The corporate slide decks had this statistic in a chart right at the beginning of a presentation, as if it should be enough to impress potential clients in its own right, without any further explanation. I wasn't comfortable presenting it in that way. So, I still used the chart, but I put it at the end of the presentation, after describing the benefits that our technology brought to our clients. I explained that our focus on meaningful benefits had put us into the number one position. The 'we are number one' chart went from empty boast to bona fide credential, linked to our focus on clients.

Differentiators

Our differentiators are the solutions that we provide that are rare in the market — in other words, the things that set us apart from our competition. They are the reason our clients choose to work with us and not someone else. They are the answer to the question, 'Why should I pick you?'

Differentiators may be a subset of the credentials that make you stand out. A credential is still valid even if other people have it — for example, an ISO certification is no less impressive because other companies hold it. By contrast, a differentiator is something that is much less widely held or achieved.

There are two key pitfalls to look out for when defining your differentiators.

The first is overestimating 'uniqueness'. Unless you are in a niche industry and/or have a 100% unique offer, there is a good chance that there will be other companies out there who do what you do. I have seen many examples of communication where companies talk about things like their 'unique methodology'. Remember, the word unique is an absolute — it literally means that no one else in the world does what you do or has what you have. Unless you know that to be an incontrovertible fact, it is wise to avoid the word 'unique'. (Furthermore, I find it hard to see how any methodology can be truly 'unique'.)

The second pitfall is underestimating our own value or skills. We often assume that what we know is common knowledge or common sense. We think that 'surely everyone can do this', when in reality, our offer is less common than we think. It can be difficult to see ourselves as others see us — it is similar to trying to write our own CV or LinkedIn profile. We're too close to form an objective assessment of our abilities.

A useful technique for understanding your strengths is to ask your existing clients for their feedback. Most happy clients are willing to provide input, and if you structure the questions well, you will gain some valuable insights. This process works better if you don't ask for a large time commitment from them. Try to limit your questionnaire to seven questions or fewer.

Clients are often more forthcoming if you are not the one directly asking the questions, so consider asking a third party to conduct the interviews and record the answers. You can also ask the third party to anonymise the information to make your clients feel even more comfortable with the process. I've been on both sides of this process and truly believe in its value. It is worth taking the time to explore and develop your differentiation, and asking for external validation is a tried-and-true method.

Remember, when you are analysing your credentials and differentiators, think as broadly as possible — there may be aspects of your solution that your customers value as credentials that you have not previously considered.

DIFFERENTIATION/CREDENTIALS

- VALUES-ENVIRONMENT, SOURCING, COMMUNITY, SUSTAINABILITY
- IP / PATENTS
- SERVICE / WARRANTY
- INTEGRITY / TRUST/ COMPETENCE
- CERTIFICATION
- SKILLS / KNOWLEDGE / EXPERIENCE
- FINANCIAL
- LOYALTY / LENGTH OF SERVICE (TEAM AND CUSTOMER)
- REFERENCES
- AWARDS / RECOGNITION
- STAFF QUALIFICATIONS / ONGOING TRAINING
- GUARANTEE / PROMISE
- TRANSPARENCY - RESULTS, COMMUNICATION
- INDUSTRY BODIES / MEMBERSHIPS
- STANDARDS - E.G. ISO

QUESTION 5: HOW WILL YOUR AUDIENCE BENEFIT FROM WORKING WITH YOU?

Benefits are the single most important part of your message, and yet they are the part that is so often left out. See if this scenario sounds familiar. You have identified your customer's issues, goals, and aspirations. You have presented your offer and described what makes your solution special. Now you sit back and think to yourself, 'That's it, job done. I've told the client everything they need to know. Surely after all that, it must be obvious to them how our offering could help their business. The rest is in their hands'. Then you rest on your laurels, pat yourself on the back for a communication job well done, and wait for your prospective clients to come knocking on your door.

Remember that there are two viewpoints — the inside out and the outside in. What seems blindingly obvious from the inside looking out is not evident at all, or at least needs some elucidation, for those on the outside looking in.

If you have answered the first four questions above, you may believe that you have your message strategy sorted. All done and dusted. Yet there is a final, fifth question that carries more weight than all the rest — how does your client benefit from your offer? Without taking this last step in the process, all your hard work on the first four steps could be in vain.

Remember those 'join the dots' drawing books that you had as a child? If you didn't join the dots, you could still vaguely identify the subject of the picture, but it was only when you drew the line, following the numbered marks, that the image came clearly into focus.

That is what you need to do for your prospective customers — join the dots. They may have a general idea about why they want to work with you, but you want to give them a crystal-clear picture of the benefits that they will receive. Paint a picture that leaves no room for doubt, one that compels them to choose you.

You need to be able to answer the following questions: What benefits do you bring compared to the competition? What improvements should they expect to see once they start working with you? How will their business be different once you have delivered your solution?

Being able to articulate your benefits joins the dots between the first four questions, connecting them together to create a complete picture. This process gives you a detailed answer when your client asks you, 'So What?'

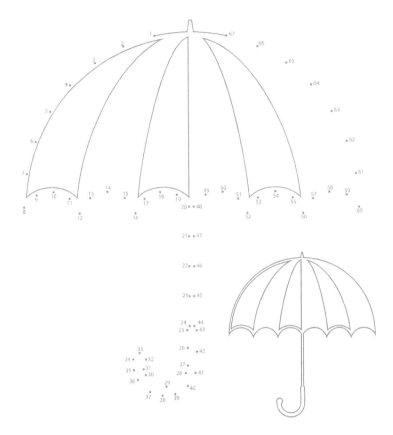

What Is a Business Benefit?

Business benefits are in the 'eye of the beholder'. A benefit for one prospective client may not be a benefit for another. If I asked you, 'What is the benefit of an umbrella?' you might say, 'To keep off the rain'. At least you would if you were in London, Melbourne, or New York. Yet what if I asked you the same question, and you were on a beach in a heatwave? You would be more likely to say, 'To keep off the sun'.

So, in order to clearly articulate the benefits your customers will receive from working with you, you need to link back to their issue or goal. The benefit, quite simply put, is the absence of the issue once you have helped the client achieve their goal.

When articulating your business benefits, be specific and stick as close as possible to your customer's issue. For example, if your prospective client is in an industry that is heavily regulated and where compliance is essential, the benefit that you offer may be that your solution will help them comply with 'XYZ' regulation. When you present your solution in this way, your client will feel confident that you understand their issue and can provide a benefit that will allow them to reach their goal.

Your solution may also include 'softer' or more emotion-based benefits. These could be personal to the decision-maker and might include specific improvements within the company. These can be harder to express in formal written communication, but you should certainly be aware of them in conversations with the client.

In Question 2 above, you will have captured your audience's strengths, and this too is important when articulating benefits. This will allow you to express the benefits of your solution within the context of the audience's capabilities and successes so far. This often resonates more with your audience than benefits that are simply linked to their problem.

The Outcome

Once you have answered these five strategic questions, you will be well on your way to transforming your communication into messaging that connects, convinces, and converts.

Understanding your clients' goals and clearly expressing your 'why' connects you with your audience, allowing your message to resonate above the noise of the crowd.

Communicating your solution, along with your credentials and differentiators, convinces your audience that you are the company that can help them.

Customising your benefits to meet your clients' needs converts your audience into loyal customers who will enthusiastically advocate for your business.

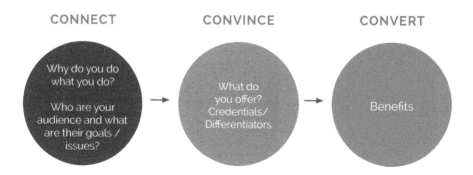

CONNECT   CONVINCE   CONVERT

Why do you do what you do?

Who are your audience and what are their goals / issues?

What do you offer? Credentials/ Differentiators

Benefits

The Five Questions

Below is a worksheet that you can use to document your answers to the five questions. You can use this as a high-level starting point to capture your own thoughts. You can also expand on it as an exercise to use with your team to stimulate discussion and reach consensus. When I run message strategy workshops with clients, this exercise takes at least half a day, and we have representatives from each part of the business in the room, usually in the form of the leadership team. No matter the level of detail that you achieve, this exercise will help you define the fundamental aspects of your message. Once you have surveyed the questions and documented your answers, you will have a foundation for your business communication. As one of my clients said after going through this process: 'It means you always know what you're going to say — you never have to reinvent the wheel.'

WHY:

AUDIENCE:
ISSUES
GOALS
ASPIRATIONS

SOLUTION:
TIER 1
TIER 2
TIER 3

OFFER:
CREDENTIALS
DIFFERENTIATORS

BENEFITS

'You Know How'

A great tool to use to check your value proposition is the 'You know how...' model.

This method summarises the client's problem and your value, using four simple statements:

'You know how' describes the problem or aspiration, and it may also include the audience's strengths. This aligns with your answers to Question 2.

'Imagine instead' turns this around and describes the desired goal, i.e. the absence of the problem. This is the benefit to the audience, aligned with Question 5.

'We offer' summarises the elements of your solution that address the issue or goal, as per Question 3.

'So you can' reinforces the outcomes and benefits one more time.

You'll see this technique used in ads, where there is limited time to describe the problem, solution, and credentials.

You can use the worksheet below to create your 'You know how' statements. If you solve more than one problem for more than one audience, you'll need a statement for each.

In this filled-out worksheet, I have used the same client example as in Chapter 3.

YOU KNOW HOW... You want to implement new cost saving technology to all your branches across the country, but you can only do a few at a time, and it's just going to take so long.

IMAGINE INSTEAD... That you didn't have to wait until one branch was finished before moving on to the next.

WE OFFER... Engineers all around the country, each following the same process and managing multiple branches in parallel.

SO YOU CAN... Finish your project in a shorter elapsed time, benefiting from the cost savings of your new technology sooner.

YOU KNOW HOW...

IMAGINE INSTEAD...

WE OFFER...

SO YOU CAN...

NEXT STEPS

In the next chapter, we'll learn how to transform our strategy into practical implementation that will reach our audience. We will explore 10 formats of business communication — from an elevator pitch to a website to a LinkedIn profile — and we'll consider how each form incorporates the 5 elements of strategy from this chapter. We will also determine how we can best utilise each format in the stages of the customer journey to help our message connect, convince, and convert.

5

The 10 Forms of Business Communication

LET'S RECAP

We have learnt what 'effective communication' means; we've seen why having a 'So What' is so important; and we've discovered how to connect with our audience using consistent strategy. So far, so good. Now it's time to start looking at the practical side of 'Connect, Convince, Convert' — that is, how do we get our strategically planned message out to our target audience? How do we use communication to take them from 'don't know anything about us' to 'couldn't live without us'?

10 FORMS OF BUSINESS COMMUNICATION

We have established that we are all subjected to multiple forms of communication every day, every hour, every minute. However, when you examine these forms of communication, you will find that, in business, there are only ten main categories, each with its own format, purpose, and role in the customer journey.

1. Elevator Pitch
2. Website
3. Brochure
4. Articles and Blogs
5. Newsletter
6. Proposal
7. Case Studies
8. Presentations
9. LinkedIn Profile
10. eBook

You will be familiar with each of these ten types of communication. You probably use most of them in your business. Still, you may be asking yourself, 'Only ten? I'm sure we use more than that'. Whilst there are always outliers, my observation is that every piece of communication falls somewhere on this 'Top Ten' list. Why is this important to know? (Or, 'So What?') Well, once you realise that there are only ten main forms of communication, your messaging becomes more efficient and streamlined.

For example, some of what you might think of as 'other' forms of communication are actually a variation on one of the ten. For example, many companies have what they call a 'value proposition' or 'positioning statement', which is a short, written introduction to the company. The positioning statement is the first cousin of the elevator pitch. When you understand the connection between these forms of communication, it helps you create a consistent marketing strategy for your business. You can put time and effort into developing your messaging, knowing that you'll be able to use it over and over again.

Grouping your communication into these ten forms lets you harness the power of repurposing. This allows you to become more organised in the way that you get your message out to your audience.

Repurposing is an essential tool in the armoury of consistent and efficient communication. It means that once you have got your message clear in a certain format, you can, with some minor adjustments, use it in all the related formats. To use the example above, the time spent on an elevator pitch also gives you a positioning statement. Repurposing doesn't mean that you copy a piece of communication word for word; however, you are able to use it with only minor changes, keeping the core of the message. It's not only desirable; it's essential for making efficient use of your marketing expenditure.

None of these forms of communication works in isolation. They form a communication ecosystem. Each format supports the others, giving prospective customers multiple paths to your company. One client might start at your website, read an eBook, and then make a decision to engage with you. Another might read your articles for a year, check out your website, read your LinkedIn profile, hear you present at a conference, and then ask for a formal proposal.

Remember the story of my son Billy and me in Chapter 2? We took different paths to cross the river, but we both got there in the end. It is your job to ensure that no piece of communication has a dead end. Each time you interact with a prospective client, there must be a signpost that prompts them to take another step, whether that's reading another article, clicking through to read a testimonial, or picking up the phone. Every communication must have a call to action.

So, in this chapter, we're going to look at those 10 communication formats. We'll consider where and how you might use them, and the role that each one plays in taking the customer on their Connect, Convince, Convert journey.

1: ELEVATOR PITCH

An elevator pitch is quite simply one of the most important business assets you'll ever have. It opens the door to opportunities that you may not even have realised were sitting within your reach.

An elevator pitch is a short verbal summary of what you do, who you help, how you help them, and the outcomes you empower them to achieve.

It is delivered in literally seconds, certainly no more than a minute, hence the name 'elevator pitch'. The idea is that if you got into a lift with someone and they asked, 'What do you do?' you could give a summary in the time it takes the lift to get to your floor. (I guess a bit of poetic licence is necessary here, and we have to assume that you are not taking the lift to go just one floor!).

There are two variants of the elevator pitch, used in different scenarios.

THE ONE-MINUTE PITCH

The first version is the 'one-minute pitch'. This is no more than sixty seconds and is typically used when you have a formal opportunity to introduce yourself. For example, you can use the one-minute pitch when you are in a business meeting or a networking event where everyone gets a chance to present themselves and what they do. You'll be given anywhere from 30 to 60 seconds, and generally you can expect that people will do you the courtesy of listening for the duration of your allotted time.

THE 10-SECOND INTRO

The 10-second intro is typically used in less formal situations, and is often in response to the question, 'What do you do?' There is no specific allotted time for your answer, but usually you'll have around 10 seconds (maybe 15 max) before it's time to pause and let the other person react.

Story

A few years ago, I was meeting with a surgeon to discuss an upcoming sinus operation. As I sat down in his consulting room, the doctor made conversation, asking me, 'So tell me, what do you do?' I thought he was just being polite, but my elevator pitch was so ingrained in my brain that it came out without me even having to think about it. 'I'm a business communication consultant', I replied. 'I specialise in helping technology companies win more business by clearly articulating the value of what they offer.'

What he said next blew me away. 'That's interesting', he responded. 'I'm an investor in a technology company, and we need someone who can help with exactly that.'

One week later I had a meeting with the company, and two weeks later I had a new client.

With that 10 second elevator pitch, I explained what I do (business communication consultant), who I help (tech companies), how I help them (articulating their value), and the outcome (win more business).

THE ROLE OF AN ELEVATOR PITCH

The elevator pitch sits very firmly in the 'Connect' stage of communication. It is part of that first step of the customer journey, helping prospects discover you and learn what you do. The sole job of an elevator pitch, whether it lasts 10 seconds or one minute, is to elicit curiosity. If you hear, 'That's interesting, tell me more', or 'How do you do that?' or 'I must introduce you to John, he's interested in that', then you know you've done a good job.

A good elevator pitch creates opportunity, but that doesn't mean that it blows the door wide open. It may be just the tiniest chink. My surgeon didn't sign up there and then for my services, but he was interested enough to introduce me to someone else. I then took the other party through the 'Convince' and 'Convert' stages of the customer journey. Without that elevator pitch, I would have had beautifully straight sinuses, but no new client. I wouldn't even have known that the opportunity was there. A door would have been firmly slammed shut.

2: WEBSITE

Think about the very first time your existing clients became aware of you. If it wasn't face to face, there's a good chance it was through your website. Even if you do meet with a prospective client face to face, once they have engaged with your elevator pitch, the next place they are likely to go is your website. This makes your website a vital part of your business communication strategy. It can reach more people than almost any other format; it is often the first place where your potential clients learn about your business; and it can be the determining factor as to whether your prospect decides to engage with you further.

THE ROLE OF A WEBSITE

From the description above, we can clearly see that the role of a website is to make a connection with your prospective clients. Yet unlike the elevator pitch, whose only job is to connect, a good website actually carries out all three forms of communication. It can — and should — convince and convert, as well.

A website, therefore, plays three different roles in your business communication, and different parts of the site do different jobs.

In modern websites, the home page and about page are the sections that make the connection. Internal pages that feature solutions, blogs, and case studies convince the visitor that you know what you're doing and can help them. Finally, downloadable eBooks inform the visitor and encourage them to take the next step on the conversion journey, along with clear calls to action, commerce pages, and contact details. When you are designing your website, it is essential to create and organise your content with these three roles in mind. Planning ahead in this way ensures that you present the relevant information at the right time and in the right place. Think back to the pyramid we saw in Chapter 4 — the home page sits at the top of the pyramid, giving the prospect information that connects, as well as a taste of the convince and convert messages. The internal pages sit in the middle of the pyramid and offer solutions that convince your prospect. The eBooks and other detailed content sit at the bottom of the pyramid and describe the benefits that the prospect will receive when they work with you, prompting them to convert on your offer.

3: ARTICLES AND BLOGS

An essential part of effective communication is the sharing of useful information. When you showcase educational content through articles and blogs, you are more likely to engage your audience than if you focus solely on advertising, special offers, and promotions.

If you need convincing, think about what you look for when you read a newspaper. I am certain that you don't turn straight to the ads. You read the paper for the information, insights, education, and entertainment that it provides. Your target audience has the same experience when they engage with you online. They don't want to be bombarded with advertising; instead, they will be more likely to engage with you if you present them with a new angle on a topic of their interest.

Blogs and articles provide an excellent format for sharing your ideas. However, make sure that they don't stray too far from their purpose of conveying information. If they become too 'salesy', your audience will see straight through them.

THE ROLE OF ARTICLES

Sharing your insights in an article shows generosity and helps to build relationships with both prospective and existing clients. Articles on relevant topics can therefore create connection, guiding your audience to your online presence through popular searches.

Articles also play an important role in convincing your audience that you are knowledgeable about your subject.

Now, I am aware that some companies believe that articles and blogs will inadvertently 'give away' their ideas. They argue that this information represents valuable intellectual property, which customers should pay for, and they don't want to give it away for nothing.

I'm certainly not suggesting you give away the crown jewels, but consider this:

If you were a chef, and you had the world's most delicious sauce, wouldn't you want to give people a taste? Otherwise, how will they know how good it is? You're not going to give them the recipe, but by giving them a taste, you increase the chances of them buying a bottle.

Articles give your audience a taste of your secret sauce. It's a great way of convincing them that you are 'delicious' without giving away the recipe.

4: BROCHURE

A brochure is a summary, typically in two to eight pages, of your value proposition and/or solution(s). It is often an extended version of your positioning statement, where you get a chance to explain your offering in more detail. It may include testimonial quotes or short summaries of customer stories. It will always have a call to action and contact details.

It is generally accepted that a brochure is more 'salesy' than other forms of communication in our Top Ten list (such as a blog article, which should share useful information without pushing for a sale). However, that doesn't mean that a brochure is simply a long advertisement — it still needs to contain information that makes the prospect want to read it.

You may think that brochures are 'old hat' and not really utilised in the digital age. Certainly, printed brochures are less widely employed than they used to be. However, they do still have a place in many industries, and a brochure can, of course, be in a softcopy as well as a printed format.

THE ROLE OF A BROCHURE

The primary role of a brochure is to convince. On your website, for example, once your visitor has connected with the high-level information on the home page, you can provide them with a downloadable softcopy of your brochure where they can read more about your solution(s). The brochure reinforces the messages on the site and helps move the prospect through the convince process.

In hardcopy, a brochure is best used in a similar role — it serves as the follow up from an initial conversation. You can leave your brochures with a prospect after a face-to-face meeting, for example. You can also give out your brochures after an initial discussion at a trade show, exhibition, or conference.

Brochures are much less effective if you try to use them at the 'Connect' stage. Since they are a tool for convincing, they rely on the 'warm-up' from an initial conversation or website visit.

If you were a chef, and you had the world's most delicious sauce, wouldn't you want to give people a taste? Otherwise, how will they know how good it is?

I'll bet that, like me, you've seen websites that go into 'brochure level' detail on the home page. Perhaps you've also been to events where a salesperson simply thrusts a printed brochure at you. I'm sure that you now understand why this approach doesn't work — the vital first step of making a connection is missing. Think of a brochure as a tangible piece of 'Convince' memorabilia that keeps you fresh in your prospects' minds.

5: NEWSLETTER

A newsletter is a generic term for a subscription-based communication. That means it goes out to people who have specifically requested it (under privacy rules in many countries, you cannot send a newsletter unless it is requested). You might call it electronic direct marketing (eDM), a nurture email, or something similar. The defining characteristics of a newsletter are:

1. Your audience has asked you to communicate with them.
2. Your communication is not anonymous — you know exactly who you're communicating with.

That means that the audience for your newsletter is quite a bit further down the track than the people finding your website or checking out your LinkedIn profile for the first time. They may be existing customers, or they may still be prospects.

They have made a connection, they've learnt more about you, and they have elected to continue the relationship. By choosing to receive your newsletter, they are signalling that they want to engage with you further.

THE ROLE OF A NEWSLETTER

The newsletter helps to convince and convert. It convinces by keeping you uppermost in your audience's minds. For new prospects, it's a great way of remaining in contact with them until they are ready to make their next move. It maintains the fledgling relationship, so they can gradually learn more about you and your solutions. They don't even have to go out and find that information themselves; it comes straight to their inbox.

For existing clients, it reminds them why they chose you and re-inforces the fact that they made a good decision. It strengthens the relationship, demonstrating that you don't just sell and move on. Your newsletter shows your existing customers that you want to continue to nurture and communicate with them.

A newsletter is effective for conversion because it's a personal way to ask a prospective client to take an action — to email or call you, for example.

Communicating to convert is important with existing clients, as well. It helps you transform them into repeat customers, reminding them why you're great and motivating them to buy again. It can also encourage your clients to recommend you to others. Referrals have a far higher conversion rate than leads from other sources. A news-letter reminds your existing clients of the value you add and makes it easier for them to act as your best sales rep.

6: PROPOSAL

If a prospective client has asked you for a proposal, they are giv-ing you the strongest buying signal possible that the deal is within reach. The business is not yet in the bag, but you are certainly close to it.

A proposal is a form of communication that is based on mutual agreement. That is, the prospective client asks you for it, or you sug-gest it and they agree to receive it. This sets it apart from a website or an article, which is a one-way communication that you transmit with-out it being requested.

I am sure that you, like me, have seen so-called proposals that are nothing more than glorified quotes. There is certainly a place for quotes, but a quote is most definitely not the same as a proposal.

An effective proposal — that is, one that has a high chance of converting and closing the deal — is so much more than a pricing document. It is an opportunity to remind the prospect of how well you understand their aspirations, goals, and hurdles. It's a chance to reinforce to them how well your solution will address these issues. Above all, it's your final moment to clearly and forcefully articulate the benefits of choosing you.

THE ROLE OF A PROPOSAL

A proposal sits very clearly in the convert camp. Your prospective client has connected, they are convinced, and they are ready to make a decision. If a prospective client has engaged to the point where they are serious enough about you to request or agree to receive a proposal, then you owe it both to them and yourself to respond in a way that respects and honours the faith they have shown in you.

As we have seen, in order to convert, you must show the prospect 'what's in it for them' — that is, how they will benefit. Yet this part of the process is too often left out of the proposal. This is like a runner who approaches the finish line in first place but slows down as they reach the ribbon, potentially allowing another competitor to break through in their stead. Articulating your benefits in your proposal is one of the most fundamental principles of converting.

Story

No one is immune to this oversight, and this is where I have a confession to make. For my first couple of years in business, I didn't include benefits in my proposals. Then one day, I was having a discussion with my business coach about the 5-step message strategy process and the importance of articulating client benefits. After some judicious questioning from her, I suddenly had a 'lightbulb' moment. I realised that I wasn't practising what I preached! Since that moment, all my proposals have clearly expressed the benefits that I deliver.

AN ESSENTIAL PART OF
EFFECTIVE COMMUNICATION
IS THE SHARING OF USEFUL
INFORMATION

7: CASE STUDIES

We all say that we're good at what we do. It's expected. In fact, you'd be pretty surprised if someone articulated the shortcomings of their product or service. Therefore, when you communicate that you are good at what you do, as true as that statement may be, it doesn't really set you apart from your competition.

However, when someone else sings your praises, the message has greater credibility and is more likely to cut through the background noise. That is why case studies are such an important form of business communication. A case study is a story that a current or former client writes about working with you. This ideal client serves as a proxy to your prospective clients, demonstrating that you are great at what you do and that you deliver the value that you promise.

To make sure that the case study resonates with your target audience, you must ensure that it is written in the customer's own words and from their point of view. The most effective technique for obtaining a case study is asking the client for an interview, using questions that prompt them to describe the process of working with you. Just like any good story, a case study has a beginning, a middle and an end. It includes the issue they were trying to resolve, the solution you provided, and the difference it has made. It is best to include direct quotes from a respected member of the organisation. You should avoid writing the case study yourself with no input from the customer. You should also refrain from rewriting your client's words from your own perspective. Furthermore, a case study is not a testimonial. Testimonials are short quotes from current and former clients. Whilst they are often extracted from a case study, it's important not to confuse the two — a case study tells a complete story, and a testimonial is a snippet from that story.

In a case study, the customer's voice talks to your audience. The greater the similarity between your client and the reader, the more the case study will resonate. The more well-known and respected the customer organisation, the more kudos is transferred to you for having them as a client. The thinking goes, 'If IBM/Microsoft/Oracle/Google trusts them enough to buy their product or service, then surely it will be good enough for me'.

The value of a case study comes from:
1. The story format — stories are the oldest and most accessible form of communication.

2. The endorsement — someone of high esteem is asserting that you are good at what you do.
3. The validation — the client's story verifies the successful outcomes that you provide.

THE ROLE OF CASE STUDIES

The case study's main role is to convince. A case study is typically used after the initial connection has been made, and it provides strong evidence that you really can do what you say you will do.

Case studies also help you transform your existing customers into loyal advocates. They remind your customers why they purchased from you and encourage them to tell others about your business. There's another bonus, as well — inviting a customer to be the subject of a case study enhances the customer relationship. According to Gartner, 96% of happy customers are willing to take part in case studies.

Case studies also play a part in conversion — there is nothing like seeing the benefits that another company has achieved to help a prospect visualise the same benefits for themselves. A relevant case study can prompt them to take the next step towards becoming a client.

8: PRESENTATIONS

A presentation, or webinar, is a wonderful opportunity to communicate your message and get immediate feedback and engagement from your audience.

Presentations are powerful for the same reason that they are dreaded by so many who have to give them — they are a direct, verbal, and personal form of communication. However, unlike the other main form of verbal business communication — the elevator pitch — the presentation is considerably longer. It can be anywhere from 10 minutes to an hour or more.

A presentation is not just a set of visual charts; it is an engaging story with a beginning, middle, and end. The ideas presented within flow logically from one to the next. Imagine if all the technology in your conference room failed — could you still get your message across? If so, then you have a good 'story'. The charts are there to help your audience by reinforcing what you say with images or (a few) written words.

Although a presentation is delivered verbally, it is helpful to think of it initially as a piece of written content. I recommend writing out a script, as this is a foolproof way to ensure that your ideas flow logically and tell a coherent story. It's also the only way to tell how long your story will take to present. We'll explore more about how to do this in Chapter 9.

THE ROLE OF A PRESENTATION

A presentation can play a part in all stages of the customer journey. It can be a fantastic opportunity to connect — after all, you are live (or at least live over video) in front of your audience, which gives you the chance to engage in a way that an eBook or a website simply can't do.

You can use facts, case studies, and even demonstrations to convince your audience about your product or service.

You can express your business benefits in order to convert, and you can engage your audience with a specific call to action at the end.

A presentation can connect, convince, and convert, all in the space of a relatively short time. However, just like a website, which also does all three jobs, it is important to understand which part of your presentation performs which role. You must include the right information at the right time. If you start (as so many corporate presentations seem to do) by diving straight into detailed product descriptions or organisation charts, you will bypass the all-important 'Connect' stage. I've even seen company presentations that started by introducing their leadership team, and I can assure you that the audience's attention span never made it to Convince or Convert. Similarly, if you don't take the time to articulate your benefits or ask your audience to take action, you're leaving your presentation hanging and missing a convert opportunity.

9: LINKEDIN PROFILE

First impressions are crucial. As business communication moves increasingly online, those first impressions are now more likely to be on a screen than over a handshake. Once prospective clients have visited your website, they will often look at your profile on the most pervasive social media platform in the world of business — LinkedIn.

I always 'do my homework' before meeting a new contact. Part of this research is reviewing their LinkedIn profile to see if they are someone I wish to engage with. Their profile gives a good indication of their expertise and what they offer. It offers a rapid first impression and shows how they present themselves.

You might ask, 'Don't I only need a good LinkedIn profile if I'm looking for a new job?' It is certainly true that even a few years ago, an updated LinkedIn profile meant you were looking for a career change. A profile was thought of like a CV, remaining static until it was needed for a job search. Things have changed, though, and LinkedIn is now fully recognised as being a networking, marketing, and sales tool rather than simply a recruitment tool.

Your LinkedIn profile is a crucial part of your presentation to your target audience. Whilst a LinkedIn profile may share some attributes with a CV (and there is certainly plenty of scope for repurposing from one to another), it plays a different role and usually contains a much wider range of information. It is more than a list of past experience and skills; it allows you to show a broader profile and to use visual media. Unlike a CV, which you send to a selected audience, it is publicly available. Not having a profile, or having an incomplete profile, sends the message to your potential clients that your business might not be ready for prime time.

'I picked you for three reasons. Firstly, I heard your one-minute pitch, and it really resonated with me. So, I checked out your website, which backed up what you'd said. Then I called and asked you for a proposal, and I loved the way it was really tailored to me. So, I made my decision' — New client

LinkedIn also serves as a platform to share articles and messages with your social network. It is a great tool for education on key industry and technology issues. By following influencers, clients, and prospects, you can keep up to date with their views, news, and announcements. Joining groups of like-minded professionals enables engagement in discussion of key trends and issues within your industry.

THE ROLE OF A LINKEDIN PROFILE

A LinkedIn Profile sits in both the 'Connect' and 'Convince' camps. You can use it to find and connect with your target audience, or they can use it to find you. Just like a good handshake or a smart presentation, your LinkedIn profile gives you the chance to create a positive, professional first impression. It is a showcase for your skills, experience, and personality. LinkedIn can help you establish common ground for communication with prospects, clients, staff, and employers. You may discover shared job history, interests, achievements, awards, and causes. The more sections you include, and the more well-rounded a profile you present, the more potential for connection you will generate. An effective profile can persuade the reader to take the next step in their relationship with you and your business.

Once the initial connection is made, LinkedIn can help you take your contacts through the 'Convince' stage of communication. Publishing articles can help establish you as an industry thought leader and expert. As you attract followers, you can use the platform to generate traffic to your company website and build leads.

Articles and posts keep you uppermost in your contacts' minds. Most LinkedIn users understand that the platform is about connection, not about the hard sell, so the articles that get the best engagement are those that educate and inform. Engaging with like-minded people through interest groups helps you to create more connections, build credibility, and establish trust.

There are some LinkedIn users who ask to connect and then immediately try to sell you something. This is pushy behaviour, and many people, including myself, will quickly sever that sort of connection. LinkedIn is about finding connections and maintaining relationships. It's a slow burn rather than a flash fire.

10: EBOOK

An eBook is the communication format you need when you want to discuss a topic or share information in more depth than you can achieve in an article. It is the 'heavyweight' of the top ten business communication formats. An eBook is typically anywhere from 1000 to 6000 words. It is laid out and graphically designed in a way that makes it attractive to look at and easy to read. It is a document of substance, and it gives you an opportunity to showcase your detailed knowledge, skills, and insights. It is not a 'salesy' format; instead, the reader genuinely learns something new, something that will help them in their business. Of course, an eBook is still part of your sales process; however, unlike a website or brochure, it is not overtly focussed on your product or service. Rather, it explains how to solve a problem, or it provides useful background information about a key topic.

THE ROLE OF AN EBOOK

An eBook helps you in the 'Convince' and 'Convert' stages. It may help you to get found, and therefore it can play a role in the 'Connect' stage too.

By the time a prospective client gets to the point of reading a longer piece of content from you, they are likely several steps into the customer journey. The eBook gives them plenty of concrete evidence, which helps to convince them of your value. It also encourages them to take the next step, which is why it's essential that your eBook include a call to action, such as details of where the prospect can go next. This call to action should ensure that if they're keen to pursue things further, they know where to go.

The content in a quality eBook is of high value to the reader. It may therefore help you to develop the relationship with your audience by saving this material for your 'gated' content. This simply means that the reader gives you their email address or subscribes to your newsletter in exchange for receiving it.

Story

Here is an example of how these top ten forms of business communication play a role in the customer journey. I was working with a new client recently, and he volunteered this information: 'I picked you for three reasons. Firstly, I heard your one-minute pitch, and it really resonated with me. So, I checked out your website, which backed up what you'd said. Then I called and asked you for a proposal, and I loved the way it was really tailored to me. So, I made my decision.'

THE TOP 10 FORMS OF BUSINESS COMMUNICATION AND THEIR ROLE IN THE CUSTOMER JOURNEY

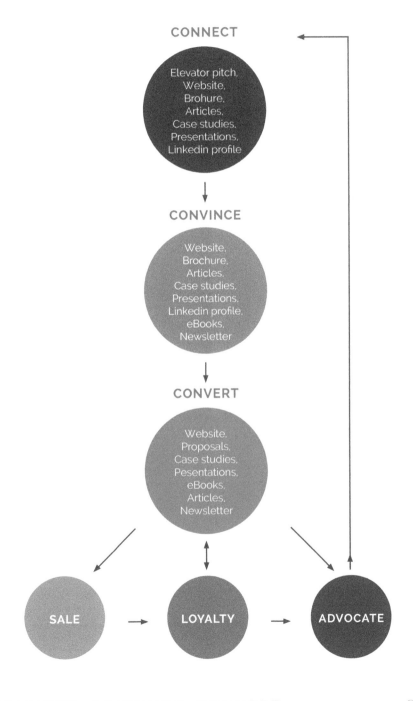

Top 3 Business Communication Priorities

Looking at these top ten forms of business communication, think about which ones you are using within your business. It may be all ten, or simply one or two.

If you are using a given format and it is performing its designated role, mark it with a 'Yes' in the table below.

Then, for the ones that don't have a 'Yes', think about which three would be the highest priority to either fix or create. What could you do that would have the greatest impact? Are you great at connection, but weak on conversion? Or maybe you're strong on convincing, but failing to make enough connections?

Choose your top three priorities to either improve or initiate, and mark them 1, 2, and 3 in the table below.

WORKSHEET: YOUR TURN

COMMUNICATION FORMAT	YES OR 1, 2, 3
Elevator Pitch	
Website	
Brochure	
Articles and Blogs	
Newsletter	
Proposal	
Case Studies	
Presentations	
LinkedIn Profile	
eBook	

Repurposing

Having used the exercise above to identify the gaps in your communication armoury, think about how you can harness the power of repurposing to fill them.

→ An elevator pitch, when put into written format, can become an introductory email or positioning statement. For instance, one of my clients used a written version of their elevator pitch when the organisers of a conference at which they were presenting wanted a short overview of the company.

→ Your elevator pitch can be repurposed for the homepage of your website to create a succinct message about who you help, how you help, and what your benefits are. The same message that grabs an audience's attention in a pitch does the same job on your website.

→ Blogs and articles can be reused in a range of ways. You can publish them on LinkedIn, include them in your newsletter, and use them on your website. You can also edit a series of articles together and repurpose them as the chapters of an eBook.

→ Presentations can be a great source of content for your articles. A client of mine recently told me that she'd created two blog articles from the content of her presentation, and in the course of our discussion, we identified at least two more potential articles.

→ The benefits that you list on your website often speak to a broad audience, but you can customise them to address the needs of specific clients, as well. Remember to include these benefit statements when you are writing your proposals so that your prospective clients understand how you will help them achieve their goals.

→ Case studies, like blogs, can be published on your website and your LinkedIn profile. You can also excerpt short testimonial quotes from your case studies to use in your newsletters and brochures.

The above examples give you a taste of what you can do with repurposing. Review your existing content and look for ways that you can adapt it. Using this strategy, you will be able to create multiple forms of business communication out of a single source.

NEXT STEPS

Now that we understand the top ten forms of business communication, what roles each one plays, and where there may be gaps in messaging, it's time to start creating some content. In the next three chapters, we're going to learn techniques that we can implement to ensure that our content connects, convinces, and converts.

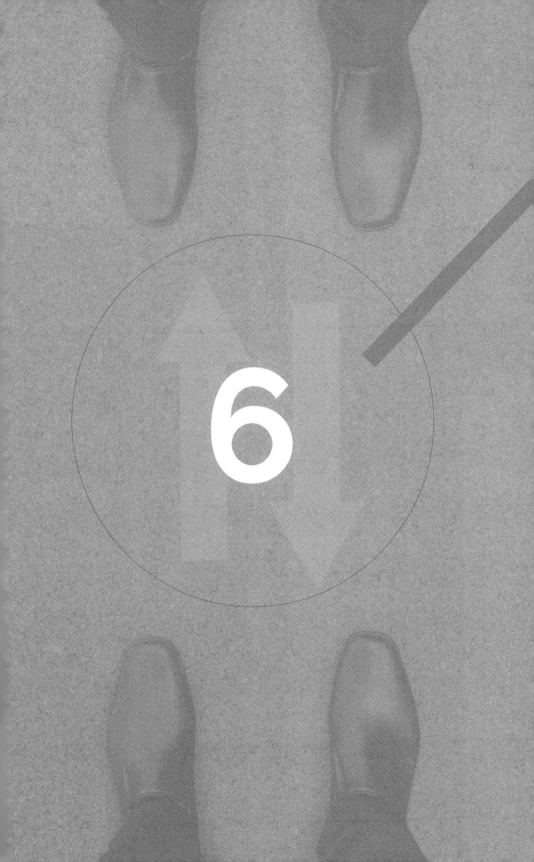

6

Communicate to Connect

LET'S RECAP

We are now familiar with the Connect, Convince, Convert process. We know how these three stages of the customer journey turn the prospect into a loyal advocate, creating a spark that builds to a flame and then a furnace. Now it's time to take a deeper dive. In these next three chapters, we'll look at the practical ways to create communication that connects, convinces, and converts.

COMMUNICATING TO CONNECT

In this chapter, we'll explore strategies and best practices to ensure that your communication connects with your target audience. It's not uncommon, particularly in the tech industry, to feel that you need to wow your audience with your technology and show off your expertise in order to win them as a client. This is especially prevalent if you're from a STEM background, where education is primarily about facts and information. Moving into a client-driven business environment means learning to communicate in a different way than you may be comfortable with. However, unless you start by making a human connection with your audience, all the smarts in the world will not be enough to compel your prospective client to go on the customer journey with you.

JUST BECAUSE YOUR CLIENTS ARE ORGANISED IN A BUSINESS STRUCTURE DOESN'T MEAN THEY STOP BEING HUMAN BEINGS.

Even if you are in a corporation selling B2B, you are still interacting with people. Remember those chickens in Chapter 4? People will respond better to messages that are articulated in human terms. So, this chapter is not about impressing prospective clients with your knowledge; it's about learning how to put yourself into their shoes to create that all-important connection.

As the researchers at McCombs observed, 'The earlier you make the emotional connection the better, because once consumers have decided they like a particular option, the more difficult it is for them to backpedal. Their thinking falls in line with their emotions'. As we will see, fostering this emotional connection is the start of a long-term, meaningful client relationship. In this chapter, we will learn five ways to ensure that our communication connects.

SPEAKING YOUR CLIENT'S LANGUAGE

Imagine this scene — you're in a busy marketplace in a country where you don't speak the language. The conversations going on around you sound like background noise until you hear someone speaking your native tongue. Suddenly, your ears perk up because you understand what is being said. Just as someone saying your name cuts through the noise at a cocktail party, so does someone speaking your language. It's all part of the way that our brains are programmed to hear messages that are meant specifically for us.

As we learnt in Chapter 3, there are two languages in business: 'What' and 'So What'.

'What' is like our mother tongue. It's the internal language of our business. Our target audience, however, speaks 'So What', or 'customer language'. So, if we're to connect with our audience, we have to learn to speak their language. The more fluent we become, the better the connection.

If you have travelled to another country where you don't speak the language, you'll know how frustrating it can be to try and communicate with the people around you. You may get by, but no more than that. Without speaking the local language, you will always be a tourist in a foreign country. Conversations will be limited, and relationships will be superficial.

By contrast, if you speak the language, you can understand the nuances of how people think, feel, and live. The locals treat you as a welcome visitor and a friend. You may even have the opportunity to become an indispensable member of the community.

The fastest way to learn any language is to listen to it. Once you have determined who your target market is, you can begin to listen to and learn your prospective customers' language. Talk to people in your target market, read what they read, and go to the events they attend. Above all, listen to what they are saying about their issues, what they want to achieve, and what is stopping them from reaching their goals.

IN BUSINESS, WE NEED TO BE ABLE TO TRANSLATE FROM THE LANGUAGE WE SPEAK WITHIN OUR COMPANY ('WHAT WE DO') TO THE LANGUAGE WE SPEAK TO OUR CLIENTS ('HOW WE HELP').

I have seen this so many times in corporate life, and I see it now with my clients — too often, we are unaware of these two distinct languages, and we don't realise that we must speak each one at the appropriate time.

HOW TO KNOW WHICH LANGUAGE TO SPEAK

Once you understand that there are two languages in business, you can ensure that you speak the correct language in the appropriate situation. If I go to Germany and speak French or go to Japan and speak Indonesian, I'm not going to be communicating effectively. In the same way, it is important to reserve your internal language for internal situations and ensure that when you communicate with potential clients, you speak to them in words they understand. One of the most common traps in business communication is to slip into your internal language in front of the customer instead of switching to theirs.

As we will see, there are several common ways that you might accidentally speak internal language in front of your clients.

SPEAKING THE 'WRONG' LANGUAGE

INTERNAL	CUSTOMER
Company goals	Customer goals
Revenue/profit/market share	Market needs
Jargon	Plain English
Offers for new clients	Loyal customers
Features	Benefits

COMPANY GOALS vs. CUSTOMER GOALS

A mission statement is an example of a company goal. It is also an excellent illustration of internal language. Let's say your mission is to be the market leader, or to double your revenue over the next year. These are great goals to share with your employees or investors, but is this really what your clients want to hear?

If your mission statement is expressed in internal language, it's not something that is appropriate to share on your website or in a presentation for clients or prospects. Yet I can't tell you how many companies I have seen sharing this internal information.

Your clients want to hear that your aims and goals relate to them. For example, they want to hear that:

→ Your goal is for every client to be satisfied or you'll offer a refund.
→ You are aiming for a 100% on-time delivery.
→ You intend to reduce cost and pass the savings on to your clients.
→ You want your clients to get a faster ROI using your products, such as reduced costs or increased productivity.

I was working with a client on the communication around launching a new product, and I asked him to explain the rationale for introducing it. 'Well', he said, 'we can buy it cheaper and make more profit'. I clarified that this was not an appropriate message for the customer launch material. He quickly grasped the point and reworded his message to explain how this new product complemented the company's existing range and filled a gap in the market. Both statements were true, but only one was in customer language.

You have probably seen another example of unintentional internal language on LinkedIn. People will often state in their profile that they are a 'high achiever', that they 'exceed sales targets', or that they are 'driven and ambitious'. If that person's primary goal is to secure a new role, perhaps their message will resonate with prospective employers. Maybe you have written something similar in your LinkedIn. There's no shame in that; however, remember that the primary audience looking at your profile will be your prospective customers and current clients. Unless you are in the market for a new job, an employer-oriented profile may not benefit you. Instead, ask yourself, what is the most important thing that prospective customers need to read about you? Is it that

The earlier you make the emotional connection the better, because once consumers have decided they like a particular option, the more difficult it is for them to backpedal. Their thinking falls in line with their emotions.

you make your sales targets? Or is it that you understand the issues that your customers face and know how to solve them? The LinkedIn message about sales targets is a prime example of internal language, whereas a message that focusses on helping clients is customer language, or 'So What'. Articulating customer goals in this way shows your clients that you understand their issues, you know how to address their problems, and you will improve their business if they choose you.

JARGON AND ACRONYMS

Every industry has its own jargon and acronyms — words and expressions that are instantly recognisable to those in the industry, but complete mumbo jumbo to those outside. As the dictionary puts it, these are 'special words or expressions used by a profession or group that are difficult for others to understand'.

This 'specialist language' plays a useful function inside a business or organisation. It is a 'shorthand', a way of talking about something without having to spell it out in full every time.

JARGON CAN BRING LIKE-MINDED PEOPLE TOGETHER, GIVING THEM A SENSE OF ALL BEING PART OF THE SAME TEAM.

If you and your client are in the same 'club', and you both use and understand the same jargon, then it can be a positive form of communication. It reinforces your bond, building a relationship and enhancing a sense of community. It can show that you are part of the same 'tribe' as them, and that you understand their industry and issues. However, if your ideal client is not in the bubble of your linguistic community, using jargon may make them feel like an outsider. They are less likely to understand you or feel that you understand them. To avoid this communication barrier, you need to speak your client's language.

If you're connecting in a one-to-one situation — that is, with a single person or company — and you are absolutely sure of the jargon or acronyms they use, then go for it. However, a word of warning — this approach only works for individualised communication. When you are using mass forms of communication (think websites, articles, case studies, eBooks, etc.) where you cannot be sure who is going to read your message, my advice is to avoid jargon unless you are 100% certain it will be understood. Furthermore, use a sensible approach to acronyms. The commonly accepted practice is to write the words out in full the first time you use them, followed by the acronym in brackets. After that, you can use the acronym on its own, knowing that your audience can always refer back.

IF YOU SPEAK IN NON-JARGON, THERE IS NO RISK. EVERYONE WILL UNDERSTAND YOU.

If you use jargon that has no meaning for your target audience, you risk alienating a percentage of your prospective customers before a connection is even made. To someone who is not 'in the know', jargon is frustrating, annoying, and a sure way to get them to disengage with you. The opposite of jargon is Plain English — that is, English that is clear, understandable by non-experts, and easy to read.

DIFFERENT VERSIONS OF ENGLISH

George Bernard Shaw described the UK and the US as 'Two nations divided by a common language'. British and US English differ in their 'correct' forms. Other English-speaking countries, like Australia, Canada, and Singapore, have their own forms, as well, which are largely based on the British and US formats.

If your communication is targeting a particular English-speaking audience, be aware that they might not feel that you're speaking their language if you use the grammar and spelling standards of another country. In the UK, for example, some people resent being addressed in US English and feel that it's an indicator of carelessness and inaccuracy. Conversely, some people in the US view the use of UK English as a sign of arrogance. There are others, of course, who don't mind either way, but you're not going to know who they are, so I recommend addressing Australian, British, and US English audiences with their respective linguistic standards.

PRICING AND OFFERS

If you're a regular customer of a product or service, how do you feel when you see a special offer available only to new clients? I know that I think, 'Hang on, I've been buying your product for years. Where's my discount?' Those offers are based on internal thinking and language. By focussing on winning new customers rather than looking after existing ones, they are expressing an internal goal — that acquiring new customers is the top priority. You may even have done this yourself, thinking that the message will resonate well with potential new clients, but there are two downfalls to this approach:

Firstly, a connection made purely on the basis of a discounted price does not have a strong foundation and is unlikely to stand the test of time.

Secondly, this type of offer risks sending a message to long-term customers that you don't care about them.

For example, a family member of mine had been subscribing to *The Age* newspaper for over thirty years. One day, he saw an advertisement offering a luxury hamper to new subscribers. He wrote to the paper, telling them that it felt like a 'kick in the teeth' to see new customers being rewarded when he, a longstanding and loyal customer, was made no offer. (All credit to *The Age* — they sent out a hamper to him the next day.)

FEATURES VS. BENEFITS

The best example of internal versus external language is the difference between features and benefits.

FEATURES TEND TO BE INTERNAL LANGUAGE, WHEREAS BENEFITS ARE ALWAYS CUSTOMER LANGUAGE.

Many organisations, especially those with a technical product, love talking features. Speeds and feeds. Pricing. Size. The fastest processor. Features are much easier to talk about than benefits. They are part of the product, and they don't change from client to client. We learn them easily, and we can quote them on our brochures and our websites. They are a temptingly simple tool to use, and so we often fall into the trap of thinking that features have value in their own right. However, features have no inherent benefit unless someone has a problem that can be solved by the specific feature.

Customers want benefits; they want to know how your product or service will solve their problem and change their life. This is why benefits are much harder to articulate. To talk benefits, you need to know your client inside and out. The same feature may have different benefits for different people. A particular feature may deliver no benefit to client A but massive benefit to client B.

I once worked with a sales rep who was very keen to explain to a prospective client the superiority of his organisation's support service. 'We guarantee that we'll respond to your service call in two hours', he wrote in a tender response, 'and that we'll have an engineer onsite in four hours if we can't fix the issue over the phone'. He was confident of winning the client's business, knowing that this was a much faster response time than his competitors could offer. What he didn't realise, however, was that he was describing a feature without considering whether it offered a benefit for his customer. Indeed, he didn't win the contract. The client offered a debrief to explain why: 'You talked about how quickly you would fix a broken machine', she explained, 'but I'm not nearly as interested in how fast you'll fix it as I am in knowing that I won't have to call for support in the first place. I'm looking for a supplier who can provide me with machines that are highly reliable. Once a machine has failed, my business is in trouble'.

If the seller had sought to understand what benefits the client was looking for, he would have realised that the speed of response wasn't a benefit to that client. Instead, he should have been focussing on the reliability of the product.

THE SIMPLEST WAY TO TRANSLATE FEATURE TALK INTO BENEFITS LANGUAGE IS TO ASK, 'SO WHAT?' OR, 'WHAT DOES THAT ENABLE THE CLIENT TO DO?'

For example, let's say that a feature of your product is that it has the latest processor. Is that simply a 'nice to have', or does it translate to a real benefit? An example of the processor being a benefit might be that your product will be supported by the next three versions of the operating system or application software, which will save the client the time and expense of upgrading over the next three years.

Sometimes a feature is just a feature, and it doesn't actually deliver a benefit to the customer. If you have the fastest processor available, but your customer's application can't utilise that speed, then your processor speed simply remains a feature. It doesn't necessarily translate to a benefit unless the customer needs or wants that feature.

The takeaway here is that features are specific to a product, whereas benefits are specific to the customer. Of course, there is a time and a place for sharing features with the customer, but only if they have a direct benefit. Don't confuse the potential customer with features that don't pertain to them, or you may lose the sale, like the story of the sales rep that I described above. Instead, take the time to familiarise yourself with the needs of your customer so that you can customise the description of your benefits to their needs.

CONNECTING WITH EMOTION

The connect stage of the client journey is based on emotion, as the McCombs research showed. So how do you connect emotionally with your potential customers? The answer is by sharing not just what you do, but more importantly, *why* you do what you do. Emotional connections are built on shared values. They have a foundation of respect, authenticity, and trust. So, to connect, you need to speak with admiration, passion, and maybe a little humour.

Understanding why we do what we do is not necessarily easy. Some people 'fall' into their business or their job, but there is usually an underlying passion of some sort, even if it isn't at first obvious. Sometimes we need someone else to help us articulate it. Once you get down to the real 'why' behind your business, and you start to communicate it authentically, you will draw people to you emotionally and build a connection that drives decisions.

I like the following tip from business leadership coach Ali Brown. She says that to figure out what you are passionate about, ask yourself, 'What did I love to do when I was twelve years old?'[1] It is a useful technique for understanding your own motivations. I tried this on myself, and here is what I found. At age twelve, I already loved languages, and I found fulfilment in helping people foster communication. I loved the idea that by speaking another language, I could communicate with a whole new set of people or act as a translator to help one group understand another. Now in my career, I help technology companies translate their message from 'What' to 'So What'. My 'Why' has become very clear.

I love watching the TV show 'Shark Tank' (you might also know it as 'Dragon's Den', depending on which part of the world you're in). On one episode, I was struck by a young entrepreneur who had built a successful online fashion business. She was asked about what drove her to start the business at the young age of fifteen. She described how she dropped out of school because she felt like she just didn't fit into the system. She suffered from depression and had to do something to give herself a purpose. She had tears in her eyes as she told the story. She was completely genuine and open, and — BANG — the emotional connection was there with every Shark in the room.

---

[1] Khoo, Valerie. 'Your passion story'. *Power Stories: The 8 Stories You Must Tell to Build an Epic Business*. Wiley, 2012, pp 27-42.

I recently came across a company that was brilliant at connecting with emotion. I was interviewing them for a case study for one of my clients. They install high-tech, self-service basketball 'shooting rooms' in disused squash courts. They have well-structured membership packages, and they use a lot of technology — from ball return systems to AI for shot tracking. However, their positioning statement doesn't mention any of that. Instead, their message is all about their love of basketball, their ethos of equality, and their belief in sport as a means of providing opportunity for young people: 'We love shooting hoops. No matter who you are, who you choose to love, what God you believe in, how old you are, or where you come from — we want to share our love for this sport with everyone.'

That's got to be one of the best 'connect with emotion' statements I've ever heard. (And I wish I had written it!) It instantly creates a connection with people who share those beliefs, and it forms the starting point for a long and strong relationship with their members.

The key is to be completely authentic, showing who you are and what drives you. Fakes in this game can be spotted a mile off, and the only way to build an emotional connection is to give a little of yourself. So, if you can communicate your message with passion, humour, and empathy, you will be heard by your audience's 'emotional brain', the place that actually makes the decision.

TAILORING YOUR MESSAGE

We've talked about finding your audience, but the reality is that you are likely to have audiences — plural. They may be from different industries, and they likely have different goals, aspirations, and issues.

Remember the cocktail party we talked about in Chapter 4? We learnt that the more specific you can be about who you are talking to, the more likely they will be to hear you. So, if you want to connect with your prospective customers, it is essential to target your message to each specific audience. I see many organisations falling into the same trap of declaring that 'We help everyone', or 'We meet all your needs'. However, no one thinks of themselves as 'everyone', therefore no one will think that your message is meant for them if it is also targeted at everyone else

A message that is too broad will fail to make a connection. If you have multiple audiences, you will need to create multiple messages.

CUSTOMERS WANT BENEFITS; THEY WANT TO KNOW HOW YOUR PRODUCT OR SERVICE WILL SOLVE THEIR PROBLEM AND CHANGE THEIR LIFE. THIS IS WHY BENEFITS ARE MUCH HARDER TO ARTICULATE. TO TALK BENEFITS, YOU NEED TO KNOW YOUR CLIENT INSIDE AND OUT. THE SAME FEATURE MAY HAVE DIFFERENT BENEFITS FOR DIFFERENT PEOPLE. A PARTICULAR FEATURE MAY DELIVER NO BENEFIT TO CLIENT A BUT MASSIVE BENEFIT TO CLIENT B

There will still be commonalities between them, but you will need to tweak your message to resonate with different sets of ears.

If you want proof of this, just think about the last time you sent a group email, a 'Dear all'. How many people responded? Not many, I suspect. When you send a message to a group with no personalisation, it is easy for each person on the list to ignore you because the message doesn't feel like it is meant for them. However, if you send a custom email to a specific person, you are more likely to engage their interest and get them to respond to you.

ONCE YOU HAVE IDENTIFIED YOUR DIFFERENT AUDIENCES, YOU CAN ADDRESS EACH OF THEM WITH A PERSONALISED MESSAGE ON THE HOME PAGE OF YOUR WEBSITE.

Each audience can then click through to specific, tailored information that is addressed to them. I took this approach with a client who developed software for the retail industry, but had six sub-segments, such as grocery stores, bakeries, and butchers. We structured the website with six icons on the home page, each denoting a different category. Customers could click through to underlying pages that contained specific messages about the particular challenges of each industry. The grocers, butchers, and bakers each knew that my client understood them without having to read a whole heap of general information, or worse, information about other industries that felt irrelevant to them.

Other examples include having several versions of a brochure, each for different prospective clients; or seeking out case studies that resonate with each of your audiences.

Once you start looking, you can find numerous instances of this type of precise communication. One example I've noticed recently, albeit not in the technology space, is the way in which the beauty company L'Oréal has positioned their skin moisturiser range. L'Oréal's range has five categories of products, one each for women in their 20s, 30s, 40s, 50s, and 60+, with the messaging centred on the different needs of skin at each age. L'Oréal's aim is clearly for the women in each category to feel understood and therefore be more likely to hear the message. Of course, this doesn't stop people outside those categories from buying the products. Men may buy the product as a gift for a woman, men may buy the product for themselves, women with 'young skin' may buy a product from the next age category down

— you get the picture. However, the targeted connection persuades potential customers within each category that there is a message specifically for them, which makes them more inclined to listen.

Story

Like you, I'm sure, I get approached on LinkedIn by a lot of people I don't know. Many of these individuals invite me to buy their product or services. 99.9% of the time, I ignore them. One time, however, I received a message from a Virtual Assistant who specialised in building newsletters for consultants in Melbourne. How precise and specific is that? I am a consultant, I was based in Melbourne, and I was starting a newsletter. I figured that if her service was designed for that exact niche, the niche in which I sit, then she would have something for me. So, I looked at her profile, and I saw that we had a lot in common in our professional backgrounds. It was enough to convince me to respond — for the first and (so far) only time. What is interesting, however, is that I didn't end up using her services. Whilst she had made an excellent connection, when

The key is to be completely authentic, showing who you are and what drives you. Fakes in this game can be spotted a mile off, and the only way to build an emotional connection is to give a little of yourself. So, if you can communicate your message with passion, humour, and empathy, you will be heard by your audience's 'emotional brain', the place that actually makes the decision.

I contacted her for more information, she was slow to respond, and her email back didn't fill me with confidence. This illustrates a key lesson that we have been learning about effective communication — you need all three elements (Connect, Convince, and Convert) in order to win business. This VA made a great connection, but she failed to convince me, and therefore she never arrived at the convert stage of the process.

HOLDING A MIRROR TO YOUR CUSTOMER'S GOALS

Some businesses seem to believe that sales is 'all about them', that is, they love to tell people how great their company or product is.

This seems to be particularly true on websites. Go check out a few and see for yourself just how many homepages shout 'me, me, me'. The first words you read are all about the company, its products, its services, and its history. Some of this may be appropriate and useful information, but only when presented at the right time. What these companies are missing is the single most important part of the message — the customer.

To forge a connection with you, your prospective customer first needs to know that you are the right company for them. In this initial introduction, they don't need to know how great you are for someone else, how many awards you've won, or how fast/clever/function-rich your products are. They have to be able to recognise themselves — their strengths, goals, and issues. If they see themselves as your target audience, you have a far greater chance of keeping them on your website long enough to read about how they will benefit from working with your company.

It's the same in every form of communication, from presentations, to face-to-face sales meetings, to brochures, to LinkedIn profiles, to proposals.

IF YOU WANT TO CONNECT, IT IS IMPORTANT THAT YOUR AUDIENCE 'SEE THEMSELVES' IN YOUR COMMUNICATION.

Once they do, they will know that you are talking to them, and they will be open to receiving your message.

Think about that cocktail party from Chapter 4. Let's say you have met somebody at the party, and you have struck up a conversation with them. So far, they have told you a lot about themselves, but they show no interest in you. They haven't asked you any questions, and they seem fixated on describing the many accomplishments they have achieved in their lifetime. They could be talking to anyone; the discussion is not personalised to you in any way. I'll wager that you wouldn't spend very long talking to them. I'll even bet that you would find a way to extract yourself from the conversation as quickly as possible. It's exactly the same in business. If you don't show any interest in your prospective client, they will leave you behind and seek out a more personalised customer experience.

This is not new news of course — in 1936, Dale Carnegie observed in his classic work, *How to Win Friends & Influence People*, 'You can make more friends in two months by becoming genuinely interested in other people than you can in two years by trying to get other people interested in you.' [2]

ASPIRATIONS AND ISSUES

'Start by identifying the customer's issues and understanding their problems'. This is the mantra taught in many sales training programs (certainly the ones that I took). Whilst taking this approach is better than focussing on yourself and your accomplishments, it is not necessarily enough to make a strong connection. For a start, it's not conducive to building a relationship. Again, think about how this would play out at our cocktail party. What if the person you're talking to opens the conversation by telling you about all the things you could do better? Not very endearing, to say the least.

Rather than talking to the client about their issues and problems, you are far more likely to connect if you can elevate your thinking. Celebrate what the customer is already good at and focus on what they are trying to achieve. When you reflect back to someone what they are good at, you are sure to form a connection.

As a nontechnical example, think about how hairdressers run their business. It would be pretty rare to hear them start with the client's problems. Beginning the appointment with 'Oh my goodness, you need to get rid of that frizz' or 'That style is so dated' wouldn't win them many customers. Hairdressers are clever. They know to highlight the customer's strengths instead of pointing out their problems: 'Aren't you lucky to have those curls — let's really make the most of them' or 'What beautiful thick hair — we'll get it sleek and shining'. These may be simple examples, but many businesses could stand to learn from them. When you talk to your client about their strengths, it will give you credibility and an instant level of rapport. They will be all ears, ready to hear and receive your message.

---

[2] Carnegie. Dale 'Do This and You'll Be Welcome Anywhere' *How to Win Friends & Influence People*. 80th Anniversary Edition. Simon & Schuster, 2009. pg. 56

I did have a client who was unsure about using this approach. I recommended that he highlight his client's strengths in the opening paragraph of a proposal, but he felt that it would be seen as empty flattery. He raised a good point, which is that you need to take care not to overdo it and risk being seen as insincere. Your job is simply to highlight your prospective client's strengths and aspirations. The aim is to have a softer opening than you would if you focussed solely on the client's problems. This practice also gives you a context for the offer you are about to make, and it allows you to tie the benefits of your solution back to the client's aspirations. Aligning yourself with the client's highest-level goals, or strategic imperatives, will help you to build connection.

ALIGN YOUR OFFER WITH YOUR CLIENT'S 'BIG PICTURE' GOALS

Organisations have a range of goals with different levels of importance. They will always have low-level issues that need addressing; however, there are plenty of businesses other than you that can help them with these short-term problems. Organisations can usually find a commodity solution to this type of issue, so if you position yourself in this space, you risk turning your message into a 'me too' that gets lost in the crowd.

Organisations will also have high-level, strategic goals. In his book, *CEO-Led Sales*, author and consultant Andrew Phillips explains that the more closely you can tailor your message to these 'big picture' goals, the more likely you are to connect because you're aligning yourself to what the client truly values.[3] Taking this approach also puts you into a much smaller competitive pool because there are fewer businesses that can provide a custom product.

You can further strengthen your connection when you communicate a partnership approach, rather than a supplier approach. This shows your client that you will help them achieve their strategic goals.

Here is an example of how to communicate this type of connection: 'You're a leader in your field, known for your innovation and technical leadership. [What the client is good at.] However, the emergence of new competitors means that you find yourself struggling to maintain that position, so your strategic goal is to focus on research to reclaim

[3] Phillips, Andrew. CEO-Led Sales: The new model to transform your business. Social Star, 2021.

leadership of the market. [The client's strategic goal.] We can help you manage your business operations more efficiently and free up time to devote to further R&D, which will help you retain your market leadership. [The client's issues, how we help, and how the client benefits.]'

There is nothing in the above scenario about your product features. Not that this information isn't important, but it is not the thing that will help you initiate your communication. Your 'Connect' message persuades your potential customer to listen to what you have to say, so it's crucial to give them a reason to hear you out.

UNDERSTANDING THAT LESS IS MORE

Making a connection is not the time for *War and Peace*. If you overload your audience with information at this stage, they will perceive that communication with you is 'too hard', and they'll likely move on.

This is why it is essential to have a succinct version of your message. As we learnt in Chapter 5, you can communicate this message in many formats. Verbally, this is your elevator pitch or the opening few minutes of a presentation. In written format, it is a positioning statement, the homepage of your website, or the opening paragraph of a brochure or article.

It can be particularly tricky to get the verbal connection statement appropriately short and sweet whilst still communicating the essentials. I have seen many companies that have a succinct

Your connect message persuades your potential customer to listen to what you have to say, so it's crucial to give them a reason to hear you out.

and clear written message, yet when they are asked to introduce themselves in a meeting, they falter. Even senior executives and seasoned client-facing sellers struggle to 'say it short' when they are asked, 'So, what do you do?'

THERE ARE TWO TRAPS TO BE AWARE OF WHEN YOU ARE TRYING TO COMMUNICATE IN A 'LESS IS MORE' WAY:

TRAP 1

- You dive straight into too much detail, and you waffle without really communicating the key message.

TRAP 2

- You give a generic answer at too high a level, such as, 'We develop software', or the ubiquitous, 'We're a solution provider'.

I once had a half hour meeting with a business owner who hardly drew breath, and yet at the end, I still didn't understand what his company did. Perhaps you think this won't happen to you — after all, it's your business; you should know how to talk about it. However, the very fact that you know so much about it may make it harder to condense your message to the essential facts that a new connection needs to know in order to engage.

In a one-hour presentation, you can cover a lot of ground; however, in a ten, thirty, or sixty-second elevator pitch, you not only have to decide what to say, but (even more importantly) you also have to choose what to leave out. There is so much you could say about your business, yet you have only 150 words or so to get your message across. The shorter the form of communication, the harder it is to get it right.

RATHER THAN TALKING TO THE CLIENT ABOUT THEIR ISSUES AND PROBLEMS, YOU ARE FAR MORE LIKELY TO CONNECT IF YOU CAN ELEVATE YOUR THINKING. CELEBRATE WHAT THE CUSTOMER IS ALREADY GOOD AT AND FOCUS ON WHAT THEY ARE TRYING TO ACHIEVE. WHEN YOU REFLECT BACK TO SOMEONE WHAT THEY ARE GOOD AT, YOU ARE SURE TO FORM A CONNECTION

Communicating to Connect

Take a look at your communication formats from Chapter 5 and assess whether you are incorporating the above tips into your 'Connect' messaging.

For example, does your communication contain jargon or other terms that might sail over a prospective customer's head? Does your message create an emotional connection with your audience that encourages them to listen and engage? Have you tailored your message for different groups of listeners so that each audience understands how you can help them? Does your communication address your customer's 'big picture' goals? Can you communicate your message succinctly?

You can use the table below to note your findings and identify communications that need some work. As we learnt in Chapter 5, the forms of communication listed below are those that are involved in the 'connect' stage of the client journey. You can either use a yes/no, or you can rate yourself from 1–5 or high/medium/low for how well you use each communication tip.

	SPEAKING YOUR CLIENT'S LANGUAGE	CONNECTING WITH EMOTION	TAILORING YOUR MESSAGE	MIRRORING YOUR CUSTOMER'S GOALS	UNDER-STANDING THAT LESS IS MORE
Elevator Pitch					
Website					
Articles					
Presentations					
LinkedIn Profile					

NEXT STEPS

As you know, connection is only the first act of a three-part production, and no one wants to leave after the first act. So, in the next chapter, we will learn practical ways to build upon our initial connection, ensuring that our communication moves our audience to the next point along their journey. We are going to take a deep dive into the process of communicating to convince.

CHAPTER 7

Communicate to Convince

LET'S RECAP

We have now seen how making a strong connection with your target audience moves them along on the customer journey. In this chapter, we're going to take a deep dive into the second stage of the customer journey — Convince. This step persuades our audience that we can do what we say we will — that we are the people who can help them, and we will deliver genuine value. As we will see in this chapter, to convince someone, we must first build a relationship of trust.

COMMUNICATING TO CONVINCE

Business writer and guru Stephen R. Covey stated, 'Trust is a function of both character and competence'.

Character is *who we are* and is based on integrity and intention. Competence is *what we can do* and is based on capabilities and results.

Character without competence is like the social butterfly that everyone loves to have a beer with, but no one takes seriously. Competence without character, on the other hand, is like the super-efficient robot that people trust, but no one wants to spend time with.

As Covey puts it: 'Of course, you can't trust someone who lacks integrity; but if someone is honest but they can't perform, you're not going to trust them either.'

In the previous chapter, we looked at ways to ensure that we connect. To a large extent, that is based on our character — who we are, why we do what we do, and the emotions that underpin our business. Connection ensures that we are seen as authentic, empathetic, and able to help — the characteristics that make our audience want to engage.

However, as Covey points out, character and competence are both essential for building a trusting relationship. Character gives us the ability to connect, whilst competence allows us to convince. Character is more about an emotional connection; competence is based on facts and evidence.

So, if your communication is going to convince, your audience must believe you and trust what you say. As human beings, we are only convinced by people we trust. We tune out those we don't trust — they become part of that ever-present background noise. If we are to build trust with our audience, we need to communicate our character and our competence.

We learnt in Chapter 4 how decisions are made on emotion, then justified afterwards based on facts. Those facts include the tangible evidence of our competence. That is why credibility is so important — it reinforces the good work we've done to make an emotional connection, and it provides the facts that help our audience justify their decisions to themselves and others. Without this justification, the process stalls.

Here's the good news for all of you who just love to talk tech — this is where you get to do it. That's not to say that you simply provide an overwhelm of technical information — your description still needs to be linked to benefits. However, now that we are in the 'Convince' phase, there is a place for talking about what your product or service does. This is where you get to provide your supporting facts. These facts and figures communicate your competence, which builds the second half of the trust equation and ultimately enables you to convince your audience to continue their journey with you.

So, let's take a look at the key ways to communicate to convince.

PRESENTING EVIDENCE

In Chapter 4, we learnt about the McCombs Business School's research, which identified 'post-hoc rationalisation' — the way that we make decisions based on emotion, and then justify them afterwards based on facts.

So, if we need emotion to connect, then in order to convince, we need to present evidence. Evidence comes in the form of facts, numbers, and statistics. Well-researched and well-used evidence is essential to the convince process. This evidence gives us and our message the authority to speak to the part of the decision-maker's brain that needs to justify their emotional decision.

We must therefore learn how to use statistics, numbers, facts, and results. We need to research them and use them consistently through all forms of communication. They are extremely powerful in terms of building credibility and authority, and they ensure that our message convinces. Rather than simply using comparative terms such as 'bigger', 'faster', or 'improved', think how much more convincing you'd sound if you said '36% bigger', 'three times faster', or 'customer satisfaction ratings improved from 7.5 to 9'.

When I took on my first executive role, I received a useful piece of advice from an experienced leader. He told me to 'learn five statistics'. He said it would help to give me credibility, enhance my professionalism, and give me confidence. He was right on every count.

I researched and committed to memory some key statistics about my clients' industry issues, as well as the benefits of my company's approach and the results we'd achieved. I used those statistics over and over again, and I saw first-hand the way that customers engaged and listened when they heard these figures. I memorised the key ones so that I could drop them into customer meetings, as well as using them in more formally prepared presentations.

I used a combination of industry statistics and factual information. Industry statistics serve as a powerful way to assert your credibility on a wider level. They establish you as an expert in a broader industry context, not just about your own products or services.

My role was leading a division that sold IT for retail, so some of my facts were: 'Research shows that shoppers who are advocates of a brand spend, on average, 14% more with every visit to your store', and 'There are three ways that shoppers tell us they become advocates — they are a, b, and c'.

Facts and statistics are powerful, but there is a danger in using them, as well. If you throw too many numbers into the mix, they can become meaningless. Context can help you underline the meaning and significance of your 'evidence', especially if you can think of imaginative ways of communicating facts. This ensures that your audience is more likely to remember your evidence and therefore be convinced by it.

Character is who we are and is based on integrity and intention. Competence is what we can do and is based on capabilities and results.

Facts and figures can, and should, be used consistently throughout every form of communication — your website, your brochures, your presentations, your case studies. If you're going to show how a previous client benefitted from working with you, for example, it is much more convincing to say that they 'saved 5% of their cost' or 'increased leads from 10 to 20'.

So, do your research, find the facts, and use them. They are a powerful way to convince your target audience.

Story

In my retail role, I had to deliver a presentation that included the announcement of the company's latest touch screen. It might sound technical, but it was very much a business presentation to our sales channel. The accuracy of a touch screen has a big impact on the productivity of the retail staff using it, and the most important message I needed to communicate was just how accurate and sensitive this screen was. It could differentiate the point of touch to within a fraction of a centimetre. So, to make this more memorable within the presentation, I asked if anyone in the audience had a five-cent coin in their pocket. When one was produced, I told the audience that the level of accuracy on our new screen was the same as differentiating whether they had touched the 'I' or the 'A' on the word 'Australia' on the tiny coin. (Some time later, one of the audience members told me he thought of that example every time he saw a five-cent coin, so the analogy clearly did its job.)

Framing your facts and statistics as questions is another effective way to engage your audience during the convince process. Rather than simply presenting your audience with a fact, ask them to take a guess at it. Having to think about what the answer might be will engage them directly with the question. In this way, once they know the correct answer, they are more likely to remember and be convinced by it.

THE BENEFIT OF ESTABLISHING EXPERTISE

Presenting evidence will strengthen your message, and by extension, give you more authority. It will help you present yourself and your company as experts. Becoming a recognised and acknowledged expert is a powerful position to hold; it is a major step towards convincing your audience to engage with you. The power of elevating yourself to 'expert' status comes from the fact that you put yourself into a 'category of one'. There are other categories of one, but expert is one that is hard for a competitor to take away from you. It takes time and effort to build, but once you achieve it, you are likely to hold onto that status.

There are other categories of one — linguistically, anything that starts with 'the' and ends with '-est' is by definition a category of one. Be aware, however, that some of these categories are easy for someone else to take from you. If your positioning is based, for example, on being 'the cheapest', your competitor has only to undercut you by a cent to take your position. Any category of one that is based on a rush to the bottom — cheapest, fastest, easiest — is easy for your competition to supersede.

Expert, however, is a position that is far harder to undermine. There are many niches in which you can hone your expertise, niches which exist in the precise areas where your ideal customer needs help. If you are an expert and can use evidence to demonstrate your expertise, you will convince.

Your prospective clients have a problem and are looking for an expert to help them solve it. The clients who know they have a specific issue but have not yet found an adequate solution will value your expertise and become loyal advocates. Expertise can also significantly reduce price sensitivity, and it takes the pressure off many of the other 'objections' that prospective customers may have given non-expert providers.

Story

Here is a story to illustrate the power that expertise possesses to overcome the 'price objection'. Years ago, my husband and I were looking to buy a new mattress. We visited the same shop a couple of times and the salesperson provided us with some expert advice. We felt he was sharing his knowledge, not selling. With further research, we realised that the mattress we had selected was available online at a lower price; however, we went back and bought it from the store because we so valued the help that the salesperson had given us. We also knew that if we had any queries in the future, we'd be able to go and ask for help. That salesperson did a great job of putting himself into a category of one by elevating his presence and convincing us with his expertise.

USING THE WORDS OF OTHERS

If someone asked you, 'Are you good at what you do?' you'd probably answer with a difinitive 'Yes'. We all say that we're good at what we do. We're going to say that we understand our target customers' strengths, their issues, and what they need to change. We're going to say that we offer a solution to help them address those issues, and that it will deliver business benefits.

Here's the rub. Everyone expects you to say that you're good at what you do. You'd hardly be in business if you didn't think you were competent and weren't willing to say so. So, the truth is that stating 'I'm good at what I do' is not necessarily going to convince your target audience. I'm not saying that your audience won't believe it when you state your competence on your website, brochures, and LinkedIn profile. The point is that because everyone does it, it doesn't differentiate you or add another level of credibility.

The solution to this problem is to use the words of others. This technique will super-charge your credibility and make you stand head and shoulders above everyone else. It is far more effective to have other people vouch for you than to try and persuade your customers yourself.

I RECEIVED A USEFUL PIECE OF ADVICE FROM AN EXPERIENCED LEADER. HE TOLD ME TO 'LEARN FIVE STATISTICS'. HE SAID IT WOULD HELP TO GIVE ME CREDIBILITY, ENHANCE MY PROFESSIONALISM, AND GIVE ME CONFIDENCE. HE WAS RIGHT ON EVERY COUNT.

In a survey of business buyers, over 92% said that they were more likely to buy a product or service if they read a trusted positive review of it.[1] The words of others have a massive impact when it comes to convincing your audience that you are worth considering further.

There are three key factors that make a recommendation or referral stronger and more relevant:

1. Independence
2. Credibility
3. Alignment

INDEPENDENCE

We instinctively trust a recommendation that we perceive as independent — that is, not associated with the seller — more than we do the seller's own words. If we know or believe that a recommendation has in some way been influenced by the seller, we trust it far less. For example, my local gym offers a one-month free membership to those who introduce a friend. Now imagine if one of your friends told you how great their gym was and invited you to join, but then you found out that they were going to benefit financially from getting you to purchase a membership package. You'd trust their endorsement far less than if it were a 'no strings attached', genuine recommendation.

CREDIBILITY

The customers who serve as the subjects of your case studies must be credible in order for their recommendations to carry weight. If the person singing your praises is your mum or your best friend, they're going to have less credibility than an independent client. Furthermore, if an organisation that is serving as a reference is perceived as objectionable, they will impact your own credibility. To see the truth of this, you have only to look at the way that a large corporation will drop a celebrity endorser the minute they are involved in a whiff of scandal.

ALIGNMENT

The closer and more alike the recommender is to the audience, the more power their words possess. So, if you see a recommendation from someone who is like you in some way, you are going to give it more credence. Being 'like' you might mean that you have tastes in common, you like doing the same things, you are the same age,

1 McCabe, Kristen 'Consumer Reviews – 2018 B2B Sales & Marketing Report' G2 Learn Hub. G2, 7 June 2018, learn.g2.com/consumer-reviews

same gender, do the same job, live in the same area, or have the same interests. Alignment is anything that makes you feel, 'Well, if this person liked it, and they are similar to me, there's a good chance that I'll like it too'.

THE POWER OF OTHER PEOPLE'S WORDS

Imagine travelling to a town that you don't know well and needing to choose a restaurant for dinner. You might start by looking at the websites of the various restaurants to get a feel for the type of food, menu, and price that each one offers. However, this only gives you the information the restaurant wants you to know. So, once you've narrowed the choices to a few restaurants, you'll probably look at the reviews for each restaurant. Reviews that are less than positive will put you off, but great ones are more likely to convince you to pick up the phone and make a booking. Even though you don't know the reviewers in most cases, you value their opinion over and above what the restaurant itself says.

If any of those reviews happen to be by people you know, then you'll rank them even higher. Before you made the trip, if you had asked around to see if any of your friends or contacts could recommend a restaurant in the area you're visiting, that would carry even more weight. If you got a good enough recommendation from someone whose taste you believe mirrors yours, you might not even bother to look at any other restaurants.

This example illustrates the power of recommendation. It is a principle that holds true whatever your business. What other say about us will always be more powerful than what we say about ourselves. So, to be convincing, we should not simply bang our own drum; instead, we need to use the words of others, in the form of case studies and customer testimonials.

THE IMPORTANCE OF CREDIBILITY

Using the words of others is a particularly good strategy if you are unfortunate enough to be in an environment where your competition's way of marketing is to denigrate you. Whilst it might be tempting to get into a 'tit for tat' argument — to criticise them in return — a far more powerful and effective response is to build a strong set of customer testimonials (along with some authoritative statistics). Rather than trying to attack your competition, you can simply point to the wonderful things that your existing clients have said.

Customer stories and testimonials are not just limited to case studies — use them in your other forms of communication, such as your elevator pitch, your website, in your newsletter, your presentations, and your LinkedIn (in the form of recommendations). If others confirm in their own words and based on their own experiences that you really do deliver on your promises, you will convince your audience of your value.

Story

I recently worked with a client on refreshing the messaging on his website and brochures. I could see that my client had some great customer stories — some well-recognised organisations in banking, retail, and IT were long-term, happy clients. He had described their stories in his brochures, but he had not used the customers' own words. So, I carried out a series of client interviews, which became case studies, complete with quotes directly from the customers. These quotes became the foundation of the new website's home page. Now, the first thing that a prospective customer sees when they visit the website is a series of glowing reference quotes from the well-known and respected organisations who use my client's services. The full testimonial stories are available with one click from the quote on the home page, and the same stories were also turned into a series of brochures.

The real proof of the value of these stories came when my client emailed those testimonial brochures out to a number of potential clients. These were organisations where he'd had some contact but had never done business before. The response rate to that email was an astounding 50% — half the people who received it contacted him wanting to meet to know more.

CREATING CONGRUENCE

Congruence is when things align and harmonise, particularly between actions, words, and professed beliefs. In terms of business communication, I am using it to refer to the alignment of form with content, or the balance between the *way* that we communicate and the message that we are trying to impart.

For example, think of a company presenting itself as having a high-quality product, one that commands a premium price. If there are mistakes in the way the organisation communicates its message about that product, there is a risk that their commitment to quality will be seen as nothing more than a veneer. It could make the audience wonder if the product or service is worth the price after all.

A good example of incongruence is one that I am sure you have seen. It's the person who talks about how very passionate they are about a particular topic, but they speak in a voice that is flat and indifferent. The words they say are not in alignment with the tone of their delivery. What happens when we hear that person speak? Do we believe in their professed passion? No, we don't. The form takes precedence and is what we remember. This lack of congruence completely eradicates their credibility.

If we are to convince, we must ensure congruence between our message and the way in which we communicate it.

FORM AND CONTENT

I was asked by a client to review some of their past proposals. Their win rate was low, and they couldn't work out why.

One of the very first things I spotted was an incongruence between their words and the format in which they communicated.

Within their proposal, they stated many times that their business was 'client-centric'. Customers were very important to them, they said, and everything they did was based on client requirements. However, in their executive summary, every single paragraph started with 'We', 'Our', or their company name. In the rest of the response, half of all paragraphs began with those same words. If I were the prospective customer reading that proposal, I know I certainly wouldn't have felt like I was the top priority.

SPELLING AND PUNCTUATION

Just as facts and statistics help to build an impression of knowledge and professionalism, so too do accuracy and attention to detail in spelling, punctuation, and grammar. Of course, you may say that the most important thing is the meaning of the message; perhaps you feel that conformance to grammatical rules is unnecessary or outdated. This is a good example of asking the question 'So What'. The answer to the question, 'So what if my spelling is not quite accurate?' is that it can make the difference between being good enough and being truly convincing. Good enough doesn't command the same pricing as great. Good enough gets clients, but maybe not the ideal clients you want to attract. It can make your audience feel, 'I get your idea, but I just don't quite trust that you can make it happen'.

There are three important reasons why the rules and norms of language matter for your communication, all of which are important if you want to convince:

1. Accuracy in the written word attests to your overall attention to detail.
2. Using correct grammar and spelling increases your credibility and builds trust.
3. Changing punctuation and spelling affects your overall meaning.

ACCURACY IN THE WRITTEN WORD ATTESTS TO YOUR OVERALL ATTENTION TO DETAIL

A lack of attention to detail in grammar or spelling might be taken to indicate a lack of precision and thoroughness in other areas. What impression does it give, for example, if a technical company talks about precision engineering and attention to detail and then makes grammatical mistakes on their website or in their brochures? If you can't pay attention to the detail in your own business, how will your audience be convinced that you'll pay attention to the detail of their solution?

USING CORRECT GRAMMAR AND SPELLING INCREASES CREDIBILITY AND BUILDS TRUST

The way we use language impacts the way that others see us. We can never be 100% sure whether a potential client values correct punctuation, spelling, and grammar, but it is best not to leave it up to chance. We risk coming across as less professional if we use language that isn't polished. For some people, mistakes in our message can be a reason to tune us out. Misspellings, for example, have always been one of the easiest ways to detect scam emails because we associate incorrect grammar and spelling with a lack of credibility.

In my corporate life, I was part of a team recruiting interns. I had to sift through more than 100 applications and whittle them down to just ten for interview. My first pass through the pile was to reject any with spelling mistakes or poor penmanship. (It was a long time ago, and these were hand-written applications!) This brought it down to around seventy applications, which I then looked at in more detail. You might argue that some of the applicants with bad spelling or illegible writing could have had other strengths that would make them good candidates, but I took the view that anyone who couldn't be bothered to submit a correct and legible application wouldn't have the attention to detail that the role required.

CHANGING PUNCTUATION AND SPELLING AFFECTS YOUR OVERALL MEANING

Subtle changes in punctuation and spelling can dramatically change the meaning of your words. I'm sure you're familiar with the 'textbook' examples, such as the phrase, 'Are you there, Mother?' which carries a completely different meaning if it is spelled and punctuated as, 'Are you their mother?'

I came across a real-life example in publicity material for a conference (organised by a well-known consulting group), where something as seemingly innocuous as a hyphen changed the entire meaning of the event. It was billed as an 'Anti-human trafficking symposium'. The simple misplacement of the hyphen created the word 'anti-human', which implied that the conference would discuss the trafficking of beings other than humans. I am pretty sure that is not what they meant.

So, do be aware that the form of your communication can undermine the content — form will usually win out, and it may undo your efforts to convince.

'WEAK WORDS'

There are certain words that undermine our credibility, which affects our ability to convince.

I read a great article by Judith Humphrey, where she outlines six words that make you sound weak.[2] She lists **'think', 'need', 'want', 'guess', 'hope' and 'suppose'.** The article gives an excellent breakdown of these words, illustrating how they can damage our credibility and undermine our work to convince.

[2] Humphrey, Judith, 'Six Verbs That Make You Sound Weak (No Matter Your Job Title)', Fast Company, Mansueto Ventures, 31 January 2018, fastcompany.com/40523559/six-verbs-that-make-you-sound-weak-no-matter-your-job-title.

I have my own suggestions to add to this list of words that undermine our message. My top three culprits are 'obviously', 'but', and 'literally'.

OBVIOUSLY

If it's obvious, you don't need to say it; however, we often use this word to describe something that is obvious to us, but not obvious to our audience. Using 'obviously' implies that our audience 'should' know this, when in fact it is anything but obvious. We tell our prospects, 'Obviously, our product can help solve this problem', or 'Obviously, I've been in the company since the very beginning'.

BUT

But has the effect of negating the phrase that comes before it. We often say things like, 'I hear what you are saying, but...' or, 'I think he's got some good ideas, but...' Instead of using 'but', try substituting 'and'. 'I think he's got some good ideas, and I would like to add...'

LITERALLY

Literally means 'exactly' or 'in absolute reality'; however, it is often used when we mean 'figuratively', which is its opposite. Too often in our communication, we express ourselves with phrases like, 'I literally killed myself laughing', or 'Everything he touches literally turns to gold'.

SPOKEN LANGUAGE VS. WRITTEN LANGUAGE

We use these 'weak words' all the time, often without thinking about them. I'm not suggesting that we avoid these words altogether; however, we need to be aware of the impact that they can have on our message.

Spoken language is often more casual, outside of formal settings like prepared pitches or presentations. In fact, these usages are usually expected, or at least tolerated and forgiven (depending on who's listening!). Problems arise, however, when we fail to translate from spoken to written language. Written language is more permanent. Its standards demand a higher level of formality, and if we fail to adhere to them, we risk undermining our message. The fact is that we don't write in the way that we speak. In spoken language, we often adopt a casual tone to be perceived as approachable, especially when aiming to connect. When we write, however, we need to balance our approachability with the level of formality that the written word demands, otherwise we risk being perceived as less than credible.

ACHIEVING CLARITY

If we are to be understood, we need to ensure that our communication has clarity. Clarity includes our choice of words and the way in which we structure them. Structure makes an enormous difference to the clarity of our message. Structure in communication includes:

→ The order in which we present information
→ The use of summaries
→ The length and complexity of our sentences
→ The use of devices including:
  • Headlines
  • Summaries
  • Headings
  • Subheadings
  • Bullets
  • Highlighting

A clear structure gives your audience a sense of certainty and comfort that they are in safe hands; it reassures them that they are making a sound decision. Whereas the reaction to grammar and spelling mistakes is often overt mistrust, the response to a lack of structure may be subtler and harder to spot. Instead of immediate apprehension, lack of structure generates confusion. When your communication is unclear, your audience must do more work to decipher your message. Even if your audience ultimately understands your communication, this delay disrupts the customer journey. Unclear, unstructured communication will often fail to convince.

THE INVERTED PYRAMID

No matter how strong your message is, if your audience can't get past the first few words, the rest is wasted. If you want to convince, you must grab your audience's attention early and keep them engaging with you for the rest of your message.

This means that the opening of any communication plays an important role. It might be a title, a headline, or the first few bullet points in a list. The most effective 'attention grabbers' are problems and outcomes. So, convincing communication often starts with a clear title, followed by a summary of the customer's issue and the benefits that you provide.

You may have been educated to think of summaries as being at the end of a document. In 'traditional' or academic writing, particularly in STEM fields, this is standard. For business communication, however, the opposite is true. An executive summary at the beginning is a good way to ensure that your message is clear.

Such a format is known as the inverted pyramid, and you'll recognise it as a format used by journalists. You summarise the essential information at the top, providing a clear structure for your readers to follow. You then drill down into the supporting, 'nice to know' information.

THE WRITING STYLE CAN BE DEPICTED AS A TRIANGLE BALANCED ON A SINGLE POINT , REPRESENTING THE FACT THAT CONTENT GOES FROM THE BROADEST FACTS TO THE SMALLER DETAILS.

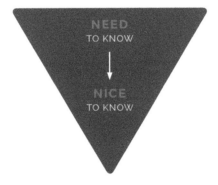

TITLE AND SUMMARY

Titles provide an opportunity to convince from the first moment you communicate with your audience. Whether it's the title of an article, case study, or eBook, those first few words can capture (or lose) your audience.

For example, I recently saw an article with the title, 'Mentoring program'. Below the title was a summary, which stated, 'The board and the professional development committee of XYZ organisation were pleased to recently share the exciting initiative of the XYZ mentoring program with our members. The program commences in October and all the details can be found on our website.'

What a wasted opportunity. Neither the title nor the summary tells us anything about the problem or benefits. This communication focuses on the 'delighted' author but says nothing about the reader. Then it directs our attention away from the article, encouraging us instead to go to a website. The icing on the cake was that the summary was repeated, word for word, in the first paragraph of the article!

The summary gave no real incentive to read on. This was a shame because the article explained that the benefit of the program was career and professional development for both mentor and mentee. This program contributed to the organisation's strategic goals and created a 'dynamic, inclusive, and collaborative' team. The title and summary would have been far more effective if they had articulated this outcome.

In the same publication, I saw an example of an excellent summary, which described a case study about a school that used pods to increase their teaching space. The title was, 'Special purpose teaching space' and the summary read, 'As with many schools, ABC College had a space issue to address. Business manager John Smith was charged with the task of delivering a light-filled, modern learning environment that blended with the school's heritage buildings, fitted their budgetary requirements and was flexible enough to meet future demands. Add to this the challenge of being operational before the start of the new term. His solution — teaching pods.'

In a survey of business buyers, over 92% said that they were more likely to buy a product or service if they read a trusted positive review of it. The words of others have a massive impact when it comes to convincing your audience that you are worth considering further.

This title and summary serve as a great example of the inverted pyramid. They give us all the key facts and encourage us to read on for more detail. The title here instantly grabs our attention by telling us the outcome that the school achieved. Notice that it doesn't tell us anything about what they actually bought — that doesn't come until the second paragraph. The introductory paragraph sets the scene, describing the problem faced by the school. Readers can understand the issues and may well identify with one or more of them.

PARAGRAPHS

Imagine reading this book, or any book, as a single block of text. No paragraph breaks, just sentence after uninterrupted sentence. This format would not be clear or appealing, and it certainly would not be convincing.

Paragraphs help to organise your message into meaningful chunks. They give the eye and the brain a chance to rest in between ideas. You cannot convince anyone if they cannot make logical sense of what you are saying.

SUBHEADINGS

If the title and opening paragraph grab attention, subheadings keep the reader engaged as they move through the content. They serve three purposes:

1. They break up the text into paragraphs, making it easier to read and comprehend.
2. They introduce each new stage of the story, acting as 'signposts' to guide the reader through the content.
3. They reinforce the key points made by the paragraphs they introduce.

BULLET POINTS AND HIGHLIGHTING

Bullet points help you convey your message in a clear and succinct format, which can increase credibility. You can also use the nested structure of bullet points to convey specific meaning. Consider the following list from a travel itinerary:

England, London, France, Paris, Louvre, River Cruise, Scotland, Australia, Japan, Tokyo.

In this format, it is just a list of places; however, if it is given structure through the use of bullets and sub-bullets, it not only becomes easier to read, but it also gains additional meaning. In the bulleted list below, we can see that the traveller is visiting England, where he will spend time in London. He will then travel to France, where he will land in Paris. He will visit the Louvre, go on a river cruise, and so on.

- → **England**
  - London
- → **France**
  - Paris
    - *Louvre*
    - *River Cruise*
- → **Scotland**
- → **Australia**
- → **Japan**
  - Tokyo

As we can see in the example above, using bold and italics also serves to emphasise key elements of your message. For instance, our traveller has bolded all the countries that he will visit, and he has italicised the Louvre and the River Cruise to ensure that they take top priority in his Paris itinerary. Be aware, however, that overuse reduces the impact of these styles, so be sparing.

RULE OF THREE

The 'rule of three' is a great technique for helping your audience to remember your message, thereby making it more convincing. The principle states that grouping things into threes is more engaging for the audience. These 'things' could be products, benefits, or target groups within your audience. Groups of three create a pleasing rhythm and pattern that the human brain finds easy to process, making the author seem knowledgeable, credible, and convincing.

Once you start looking, you'll see the rule of three everywhere — including, of course, in the title and premise of this book.

A PICTURE PAINTS A THOUSAND WORDS

The words you use form the heart of your message. Selecting the most appropriate words for written and verbal delivery is therefore crucial to being clear and convincing. Words on their own, however, can be dry, especially in written format, and an A4 page full of 12-point, black type is not visually enticing.

So, think about enhancing your words with good design, layout, colour, and imagery. I don't pretend to have expertise in graphic design, except to recognise its value in making a message clear, engaging, and appealing. You may not have read this far in this book without the beautiful design drawing your eye onwards and helping to clarify my words through style and layout. A good graphic designer knows how to balance white space, graphics, and words on a page. They know how to draw the reader's eye to the important pieces of information, and they understand how to get the reader to keep turning the pages so they will make it to the end of the text. Design is an essential element in creating clarity that convinces.

PLAIN ENGLISH

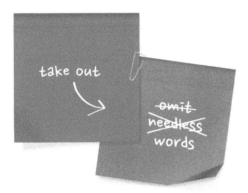

Plain English is 'clear and unambiguous language, without the use of technical or difficult terms'. It is a powerful tool for convincing your audience. Research has uncovered the following facts about the way that an audience responds to plain English:

→   Readers of all educational levels find plain English easier to understand.

→   When readers encounter plain English, they perceive the writer to be more knowledgeable.

This might seem counter-intuitive — after all, it might seem reasonable to think that by using complex language, we will convince our audience with our intellectual prowess. We may feel that the better-educated our audience, the more they will prefer complex English. However, the exact opposite is true. The better the reader understands our message, the smarter they think we are. When we communicate in a way that they can easily understand, we increase our credibility.

To illustrate this point, a study gave two pieces of writing to over 1,500 scientists from industry and academia.[3] The two pieces contained the same facts in the same sequence, and they used the same technical terms. The difference was in the degree to which each used non-technical language.

The first piece used short sentences and everyday words. The second piece did the opposite, mimicking the style of a typical scientific discussion paper. Almost 70% of the readers preferred the first document, finding it more stimulating and interesting. 75% thought the writer of the first piece was a more competent scientist and had a more organised mind.

There are numerous studies, groups, and examples that highlight the power of plain English for credibility and understanding, including the Plain English Campaign group, whose mission is to 'oppose gobbledygook, jargon and legalese'.

Research by The University of Otago in New Zealand found that short sentences generate a greater feeling of trust in the speaker.[4]

The Australian Government highly recommends plain English, and the Australian Public Service Commission runs courses to teach its staff how to write this way.

The following from an Australian Government website illustrates how the use of plain English can clarify the words in a written statement.

They suggest that instead of using a phrase like:

'If you require any further clarification or explanation, please do not hesitate to contact us by phone.'

It is much clearer and more succinct to say:

'If you have any questions, please call us.'

HOW TO COMMUNICATE IN PLAIN ENGLISH

The guidelines for writing plain English include:
- → Using short sentences (15–20 words is a good target).
- → Cutting long sentences into two or three separate sentences, or using lists.
- → Breaking up long paragraphs into multiple shorter ones.

[3] Turk, Christopher, and John Kirkman. 'Writing is communicating' revising basic assumptions' Effective Writing: Improving Scientific, Technical and Business Communication, Second Edition. E & F N Spon, 1989. pp. 14-17

[4] Owen, Helen, PhD. 'Simple sentences more honest'. Otago Bulletin Board, University of Otago, 27 June 2014. otago.ac.nz/otagobulletin/research/otago074335.html

- → Avoiding complex words with multiple syllables.
- → Taking out words that don't add to the meaning.
- → Explaining technical terms the first time they are used.
- → Converting list sentences to bullets.
- → Checking reading ease with the Flesch Scale.

The Flesch Scale measures how easy a document is to read. A score of 60–80 means that the general public will understand. The higher the score, the easier it is to understand.

You can also use the Flesch-Kincaid grade level, which shows the school grade level a reader would need to have in order to understand your content. A level 8 is understood by most people. The lower the number, the easier it is to read. The Government recommends level 5 for information presented to the public.

You can check your readability statistics in Microsoft Word — here's the score for the 'Plain English' section you have just read:

Counts	
Words	297
Characters	1,533
Paragraphs	15
Sentences	23
Averages	
Sentences per Paragraph	1.6
Words per Sentence	12.6
Characters per Word	4.9
Readability	
Flesch Reading Ease	58.9
Flesch-Kincaid Grade Level	8.1

ESTABLISHING CONSISTENCY AND REPETITION

Imagine if you came across an engaging blog article by an organisation, which really captured your interest. The article shared some useful information about a topic you'd been struggling with, and you thought to yourself that this company might be able to help you. So, you decided to check out their website, but when you arrived, you found that the emphasis seemed to be rather different than the article. You found yourself a bit confused, but you were still sufficiently interested to call them. When the company representative answered the phone, they didn't know anything about the subject of the article you read; instead, they tried to engage you in a conversation about a completely different topic. How convinced would you be that they are an organisation that can help you? Not very, I suspect.

CONSISTENCY ACROSS COMMUNICATION FORMATS

The above example illustrates the importance of keeping your message consistent across all the communication formats that you use. When we looked at the top ten forms of communication in Chapter 5, we learnt that prospective clients require multiple exposures to several forms of communication in order to feel convinced about our solution. These communication formats must work in tandem — the message in one form of communication must be echoed in another. As soon as your message becomes inconsistent, you lose credibility. Even if all of your forms of communication have a clear message and are well executed, they will fail to convince if they vary too widely in their message content, tone, and design.

You may find it relatively straightforward to handle your 'static' written formats, such as your website and brochures — after all, they are often managed centrally and can be kept aligned. I recommend taking extra care to maintain consistency across the more individualised formats, such as your elevator pitch, your presentations, and your LinkedIn profile. These communication formats may require more attention to keep them coordinated.

CAROL BENTON

NO MATTER HOW STRONG YOUR MESSAGE IS, IF YOUR AUDIENCE CAN'T GET PAST THE FIRST FEW WORDS, THE REST IS WASTED. IF YOU WANT TO CONVINCE, YOU MUST GRAB YOUR AUDIENCE'S ATTENTION EARLY AND KEEP THEM ENGAGING WITH YOU FOR THE REST OF YOUR MESSAGE

CONSISTENCY OVER TIME

Not only does your message need to be consistent across formats, it also needs to be consistent over time. Again, imagine engaging with a company because their message resonates with you and your requirements. Then the following month, you find that their message has changed, and the organisation is talking about adding value in a different way. That kind of inconsistent behaviour is neither credible nor convincing.

We spend so long with our message, and we understand it so well, that it can be tempting to think that we should state it differently each time so that our audience doesn't get bored. However, our audience must hear our message the same way many times before it will sink in. There are different schools of thought on the exact number of repetitions that are necessary, but suffice it to say, the number is greater than one. This being the case, we need to keep our message consistent over time. Otherwise, our prospective customers will hear a different idea every time we communicate, effectively resetting the repetition counter back to one. New message, new count. If we need to reach ten exposures to convince a prospective customer, it will take a prohibitive amount of time to reach this number if we're constantly starting over again with a revised message.

EXAMPLES OF CONSISTENCY

The most successful strategies tend to be long-term ones. When you are consistent, you tell the market what you offer, and what you stand for. The more consistent your message, the more it will convince your audience. Nike has one of the best-known slogans in the consumer market: 'Just do it'. They have stuck consistently with that same message for well over thirty years.

During the 'Brexit' campaign, politicians on both sides of the divide campaigned hard. The 'Vote Leave' campaign were extremely smart with their messaging. They had a simple, strong, five-word message: 'Take back control, Vote Leave'. They were clearly well briefed — in one panel debate that I watched, every single member of the 'Vote Leave' side got those five words into their answer, no matter what the question. Repeated messaging like that can have a big impact — it subliminally enters the consciousness. Whilst it didn't influence those who had already decided which way to vote, I believe it did have a bearing on the vacillating voters. When making their final decision, they may well have heard that repeated message play out in their head and followed it with their actions.

Story

Here is a story that illustrates the importance of consistency. A few years ago, I read an interesting book by a property manager, in which she described the system she used to help sellers to market their homes. She claimed that by using her strategies, the sellers she worked with were able to increase their asking price. Her book was full of useful tips, and when I read it, I felt that she would be a person that I'd love to have in my corner if I were selling my home. I enjoyed it right up until the last chapter, where the author wrote about how she also helped buyers to purchase for the lowest price. Bang — all credibility gone. This conflicting message made me realise that she was trying to play both sides of the field. Needless to say, it failed to convince me that she was 100% committed to helping sellers.

The words you use form the heart of your message. Selecting the most appropriate words for written and verbal delivery is therefore crucial to being clear and convincing.

This is why it's so important to spend time going through the strategy-building questions we covered in Chapter 4. It will allow you to build a value proposition to which you are 100% committed. Once you find your truth, it doesn't need to change. Build your value proposition and then be true to it.

Writing Convincing Letters

LETTER #1

Let's take a look at an example of many of these tips in practice. Read the letter below, and then answer the questions that come after it.

June 9th 2021
Mayor and City Council
City of Glendale
100 Glen Street,
VIC 3999

Subject: The Glenview Building

Dear Mayor and City Council,

Our firm has a problem. We have a major engineering project to develop and there is no space in our facility to accommodate the laboratory equipment that will be necessary to carry out what we have in mind. We are wondering if the city would be so kind as to help us. The historic Glenview building at Water Street is presently under city ownership, and it is our understanding that the building is under consideration for the expansion of city offices. Cheaper accommodation for city offices can be found in other districts nearby. As taxpayers we object to you using the building, and regardless of what may be planned for the building, we believe that it would meet our space requirements and would be convenient to our corporate headquarters located on First Street. Our engineering staff would be able to move quickly from the labs they have established at headquarters to a new lab in the Glenview building, our budgets would accommodate the building, and we would be able to maintain it. It would be very much appreciated if a decision on this issue were forthcoming at the earliest possible date, so if there are any further questions or comments, please don't hesitate to call me.

Tom Kendrick
General Manager
Centennial Industries

OBSERVATIONS

→ If you were a member of the Glendale council, how would you respond to Tom Kendrick's letter?
→ How would you describe the focus of the letter?
→ How would you describe the tone of the letter?
→ How well do you understand what Centennial are asking for?
→ Do you have any other comments on the letter?
→ What do you think you would do differently?

NOTES

LETTER #2:

Now consider an alternative version of the letter.

June 9th 2021
Mayor and City Council
City of Glendale
100 Glen Street,
VIC 3999

Subject: Proposal to lease and develop the Glenview Building at no cost to the city.

Dear Mayor and City Council,

Please consider our proposal to lease the Glenview building and to renovate it **at no cost to the taxpayers of Glendale.**

We believe that our proposed approach offers benefits for you and us. The benefits include:
· Restoration of a historic site at private rather than public expense.
· Renewed commercial activity in the city centre.
· The economic well-being of the community.

Restoration at private expense.
Our firm is willing to lease the property, renovate it, and turn it into a major research facility.

We understand that your current plans are to renovate the Glenview building to use as your offices. That renovation would be paid for by local taxpayers.

We are suggesting that the council could rent office space in another building, saving the public cost of the renovation and making better use of council resources.

Renewed commerce in the city centre.
Our proposed research facility would bring many new workers into the city centre, an area in need of a commercial boost, benefitting neighbouring businesses and the vibrancy of the city.

Expanded investment in the community.
We believe that private investment is valuable to a community. Our firm has a history of investment in the city centre, with our corporate headquarters on Victoria Street. The decline of this area troubles us and we want to contribute to its redevelopment.

Thank you for considering our proposal. We are confident that it offers a saving to taxpayers as well as renewed business development in the city centre.

I will contact you on 25th June to determine your decision and next steps, or, if you would like to call me before then, you can do so on 0444 123 456.

Yours sincerely,
Tom Kendrick
General Manager
Centennial Industries

OBSERVATIONS

I am sure you'll agree that the second version is a million miles from the first, in terms of clarity, appeal, and the degree to which it convinces the reader to take action. That's because it uses many of the techniques we've explored in this chapter:

→ It has a subject line (title) that instantly explains the benefit to the reader.

→ It uses the inverted pyramid structure. It starts with a summary sentence ('Please consider our proposal...'), then it summarises the three benefits, and finally it expands on those benefits.

→ It uses bullet points to clarify the three main benefits.

→ It uses bolded text to emphasise key words in the message.

→ It uses paragraph structure to explain the proposed approach to deliver each of the three benefits, with subheadings that show which benefit is being described.

→ It uses repetition, with the three bullet points being repeated in the subheadings of the paragraphs.

→ There is a clear call to action (more about that in Chapter 8).

→ The whole letter is written from the point of view of the reader, not the writer.

→ The letter is broken down into short paragraphs, with white space in between.

→ The second letter has great readability, as shown by the before and after statistics:

	BEFORE	AFTER
Words per sentence	25.3	14.4
Flesch reading level	47.7	50.4
Flesch-Kincaid grade level	12	9.8

Communicating to Convince

As we did for 'Connect', take a look at your 'Convince' communication formats, and check how well you think they incorporate the tips we've just covered in this chapter. In Chapter 5, we talked about the roles of each of the ten forms of business communication, and we outlined the ones whose job is primarily to convince. Those formats are listed in the table below, along with the tips we've just described above. You can use the table to capture how well your existing forms of communication convince, and to identify any area within your communication that could apply the tips above in order to be more effective.

Use a yes/no, rate yourself from 1-5, or use high/medium/low to assess how well you use each communication tip.

NOTES

	EVIDENCE – FACTS, NUMBERS, STATISTICS	THE WORDS OF OTHERS	CONGRUENCE – GRAMMAR AND FORMAT	CLARITY – STRUCTURE AND PLAIN ENGLISH	CONSISTENCY– REPETITION ACROSS FORMATS AND OVER TIME
Website					
Brochure					
Articles					
Case Studies					
Presentation					
LinkedIn Profile					
eBooks					

NEXT STEPS

In this chapter, we have seen how to build on an emotional connection with facts, figures, a clear structure, compelling wording, and consistent repetition of our message. These give our audience the 'evidence' they need to justify the emotional connection they have made with us. Once that job is under way, we can move on to the third phase of the customer journey — convert. In this stage, the prospect takes their next step to becoming a client. They are on their way to loyalty and advocacy — buying from us again and again and telling others about our solution. So, in the next chapter, we'll look at the tips and techniques to fan that flame into the furnace of conversion.

8

Communicate to Convert

LET'S RECAP

We've taken a detailed look at how to communicate to connect and how to ensure that we convince, so now we arrive at the culmination of the process—making the sale. Yes, conversion is making the sale, but it's also so much more than that. Remember in Chapter 2 where we described what 'Convert' means? It is getting your audience to take the next step. That 'next step' on their customer journey could be getting closer to buying from you, it could be signing the cheque, it could be deciding to buy from you again, or it might be recommending you to someone else. This is one of the big differences between Connect, Convince, Convert and a customer journey model that sees 'Decision' as a single and final step. For us, the term 'Convert' covers a wide range of possible results, the common theme being that each outcome is a step in the direction of expanding your sales revenue.

COMMUNICATING TO CONVERT

When it comes to conversion, timing really is everything. There is a fine balance between taking things one step at a time to ensure that the client is comfortable and not letting things drift to the point where the client begins to doubt whether you actually want to do business with them. When you communicate to convert, you mustn't rush, but you must also be prepared to give the customer a nudge if necessary. These two ideas may seem contradictory; however, they are part of the equilibrium of the conversion process.

The 'Convert' stage of the customer journey also serves as a 'test' of whether you have spent enough time with one or more of the previous steps. Sometimes a difficulty in converting may indicate that you need to backtrack and revisit your strategy or the 'Connect' or 'Convince' stage.

So, let's take a look at the ways in which we can find that perfect balance and ensure that our communication does the job of converting.

GUIDING YOUR PROSPECTS ONE STEP AT A TIME

Good news—if you have done an effective job of connecting and convincing, you have done around 80% of the work towards getting a new or repeat client. If you've 'marinated' with connection and conviction, conversion becomes a straightforward process. There's no extra seasoning needed.

If your audience has a connection with you, and they understand and believe in what you offer, you are well on the way to conversion. That said, there are two big caveats: firstly, the timing must be right for the client—they must have a problem that you can solve. Secondly, they must have the budget and resources for a commercial engagement. Also understand that 80% of the work doesn't necessarily equate to 80% of the time—conversion can be a slow burn rather than a fast-burning fire. As we learnt in Chapter 2, conversion is the furnace, and it takes time to get a fire burning so hot that it forges new behaviours. Conversion can't be rushed. Even though you've marinated, you often find that the process needs to slow cook. Still, we all know that slow cooking can lead to some delicious results.

When I established Words2Win, I met with a business contact from my corporate days. I explained what I was doing now and how I helped technology companies to communicate their value. They fully understood what I did, they believed that I added value, and they said they would look out for organisations that needed my services. They added, however, that they themselves didn't need what I offered.

Then a full year later, the Managing Director called to say that they were reviewing their website and other content, and he asked to meet with me to discuss whether I could help them. I had made my connection and had convinced them, but the convert process needed to wait until they were ready and had a problem that I could solve.

DON'T RUSH YOUR SALES

One of the things I found most frustrating in my corporate career was the push for revenue to meet our internal quarterly deadlines. Whilst I understand the need for accurate quarterly forecasting and planning, in the end the customer will buy when they are ready. Of course, there is often scope for a little 'push', or incentive to act sooner; however, within our system, it got to the stage where some sellers would try to get the sale at almost any cost. This eventually did a lot of damage to customer relationships and simply 'trained' customers to wait until the end of the quarter or year, knowing there was a good chance of a price drop as the pressure mounted.

TIMING IS EVERYTHING

I don't know if you believe in love at first sight, but I'm sure you understand the concept. A person walks into a room and sees the 'love of their life'—the man or woman they want to be with for the rest of their days. BANG—they just know. This person has an end goal in mind and is focussed on that final outcome. But think about it—wouldn't it come across as creepy if the person walked straight up and said, 'I want to marry you and spend the rest of our lives together' as the opening line of their very first conversation? They would stand a far better chance of achieving their goal of a lifelong relationship if they took things slowly and got to know the other person first. They need to start with some smaller steps, like introducing themselves, getting into a conversation, arranging to meet up again—you know, all the things that would make the other person feel like they were moving at a comfortable pace.

As in the example above, it is easy to become fixated on our business objectives. We want to convert our prospects to paying clients, re-engage an existing client, or have clients refer us. We are focussed on our revenue and making the sale. However, it's important to remember that our prospective clients do not necessarily have the same view of the world that we do. We're looking out onto the horizon at the goal, but they may only see the next step. So, the most important thing to remember when aiming to convert is that there may be several steps between where you are now and the final goal. It's essential to put yourself in the customer's shoes and try to understand their thought processes and decision-making stages.

> **When you communicate to convert, you mustn't rush, but you must also be prepared to give the customer a nudge if necessary. These two ideas may seem contradictory; however, they are part of the equilibrium of the conversion process.**

We all want instant action. As technology companies, you want to launch your website, send out a marketing campaign, and see an instant jump in sales. The truth is that customers buy when they have a need. You cannot force your prospect into action; you can only encourage them by making your offer clear, easy, and desirable.

In a technology sale, with a more complex value proposition, the process from lead to conversion is likely to have many proof points, each one bringing the potential client a step closer to making their decision. We need to guide our prospects through these steps to build their confidence in our solution and amplify their desire for our product. This approach eliminates the competition and brings the prospect across the finish line, completing the sale.

The time it takes to get from one stage to another varies greatly, depending on a multitude of factors, including the customer (individual or business), the product or service you are selling, the price of your offering, the complexity of your solution, the client's decision-making process, and the clarity of your communication, just to name a few.

TAKE YOUR TIME

During a summer holiday in France, my family and I spent a day at the glorious Pont du Gard. It was a scorching day, and people were jumping from a rock around eight metres high into the cool waters of the River Gardon. My daughter Juliette, who was eleven at the time, really wanted to make the jump, but she was nervous about the height. So, being the determined and logical person she is, she decided that she would have to build up gradually. We found a spot on the side of the river around one metre high, and she tentatively jumped towards me as I encouraged her from the water. That first leap gave her confidence, which grew as she found jumping off spots that were a little higher each time. Eventually, she felt ready. She went up to the big rock and finally made her triumphant leap into the river.

Likewise, whilst some clients are confident enough to make the leap the first time, others need to build up gradually, gaining confidence as they move closer to the sale. As a business, it is important to determine which type of prospect you are working with so you can adapt your strategy to meet their needs.

In the conversion process, the goal of each step is not necessarily to close the deal; often, it is simply to get to the next step. It might be scheduling the next meeting with a decision maker; it might be arranging a demonstration or proof of concept; it might even be as simple as the prospect subscribing to your newsletter so that you can continue your messaging.

Just as with the stepping stones story from Chapter 2, your prospect may take a shorter or longer route depending on their level of certainty. It's easy to feel frustrated, wanting them to take the shorter, faster route, but as with the stepping stones, sometimes going faster carries more risk of a fall. So, it's important to take things at the pace with which the client is comfortable.

If you have communicated to connect and convince, and you have screened your prospects at each stage, by the time you convert, your customers will be happy to purchase. If you have the right client and the right timing, you will find that there is a synergy between you and the client, which leads to sales, repeat deals, and referrals.

GIVING YOUR PROSPECTS A NUDGE

There's a balance here. Yes, you need to allow your target audience to take things at their own pace and choose the route with which they are most comfortable. However, if you notice that your prospect is dragging their feet or becoming distracted, you'll need to keep the momentum going so that they keep moving forward.

You don't want to be so laid back that it appears that you're not really interested in the sale, or that you're happy to let the conversion process drift along. There must always be reminders that this is a business relationship, with pointers and prompts that keep the prospect thinking of it as such.

DON'T LOSE THE HEAT

You have built up your spark of connection, fanned it into a flame by convincing, and now you have a furnace that is ready to convert. A furnace is used to shape otherwise rigid materials. Blacksmiths use the heat of their furnace to mould iron. Yet a furnace is only effective if it maintains the right temperature. If the blacksmith does not tend to their forge, it will eventually lose its heat. As the fire cools, less and less change can be wrought.

The art of conversion, like the art of the blacksmith, is to 'strike while the iron is hot' by recognising the right moment when the heat is at its highest. We must use that heat to 'shape' our audience's actions. If we don't 'strike', we risk abandoning our iron before we can shape it into something useful, like a ploughshare or a horseshoe. In other words, we have connected with our prospect, and we have convinced them of our offer, but we have walked away before we can convert them to the benefits of our solution.

So, if we are to convert, we must identify the optimum heat that creates our tipping point. This is the point at which the gentlest of pressure will tip the balance in our favour. At that point, we can apply the final nudge.

At the Pont du Gard, Juliette worked her way up to the high rock in her own time. She made up her mind to jump, but there was still a bit of hesitancy. Although we knew she'd eventually take the leap, we didn't want to wait hours for her to do it. It was the end of the day, and the rest of our group was looking forward to going home for a cool drink. Juliette wanted her moment of glory captured on video, so I told her that my phone battery was down to 3% (which was completely true). If she didn't jump soon, there'd be no video evidence. It did the trick, and that final (metaphorical, not literal!) nudge got her off the rock and into the water.

In a similar fashion, when that Managing Director called me a year after my initial discussion with his team, I arranged the meeting with him promptly. I discussed his requirements and then sent a detailed proposal, including a timeline. Once he was ready, I didn't delay. The final conversion happened within a matter of days.

WE ALL WANT INSTANT ACTION. AS TECHNOLOGY COMPANIES, YOU WANT TO LAUNCH YOUR WEBSITE, SEND OUT A MARKETING CAMPAIGN, AND SEE AN INSTANT JUMP IN SALES. THE TRUTH IS THAT CUSTOMERS BUY WHEN THEY HAVE A NEED. YOU CANNOT FORCE YOUR PROSPECT INTO ACTION; YOU CAN ONLY ENCOURAGE THEM BY MAKING YOUR OFFER CLEAR, EASY, AND DESIRABLE.

A NUDGE IS NOT A PUSH

When we are in the final stages of the customer journey, it is important to understand the difference between a nudge and a push. A nudge is the final piece of encouragement that the prospect needs to take a step that they want to take, and that they were going to take anyway. A push, however, is an act of coercion. If we push our prospect into becoming a customer, we may get them to make a purchase that they are not comfortable with, and in doing so, they may come to regret their decision.

Think about this distinction from your own experience. If you are given a nudge to purchase something that you want to buy, you will feel grateful for the encouragement to take the final step. With a nudge, you are still in control of the transaction, and you feel certain that you have made a good business decision.

The relationship goes both ways. When you are ready to buy, you want to know that the company is ready for your business. A nudge gives you the confidence to engage in future deals with the same company.

Imagine, however, if the company were to cajole you into making the purchase. Instead of giving you a nudge, the company pushed and pushed until they wore you down; finally, you agreed to the sale just to get them to stop. You would probably feel uncomfortable, and you wouldn't want to engage them again.

To give you another perspective, recall the story of my daughter and her jump into the River Gardon. Imagine if instead of encouraging her and letting her build up confidence in her own time, I had simply dragged Juliette up to the top of the rock and pushed her in. It is true that her immediate goal of getting from the rock into the water would have been achieved; however, she would have felt manipulated and unsafe. By missing out on the confidence-building steps, the chances are high that she would have avoided taking such leaps in the future, and she might have lost her trust in me altogether.

WHAT DOES A NUDGE LOOK LIKE?

There are many ways to apply a nudge. A nudge could be as subtle as switching the language you use; instead of referring to 'if' you work with the prospective client, talk about 'when' you engage.

It might be tailoring your offer to your prospective client so that the benefits you provide precisely meet their needs (but definitely not a 'something for nothing' price reduction).

It might be a final recap of the benefits, reminding your audience about the way that their business will be different if they engage with you.

A nudge might be as simple as keeping in touch with your prospects and checking in on their progress. There has been many a conversion lost because the seller simply lost heart and gave up. Research shows that 60% of purchasers say 'no' four times before they say 'yes'. Yet amazingly, nearly half (48%) of all sellers don't even follow up once.[1]

Consider the opposite of the 'love at first sight' example from above. Instead of shocking their prospective partner with a proposal of marriage on their first encounter, imagine if the Romeo in question took their companion out for a nice dinner date. Then for the entirety of the following week, they didn't so much as call or send a text message. Their date would be justified in thinking that they weren't very interested, and they would probably move on.

In a business situation, it's important not to lose sight of the fact that we are still interacting with people. Whilst our client is a business, it is made up of individuals, each of whom has feelings and all the human behaviours that determine successful interactions.

The key point of the nudge is to find a balance between letting the customer take their time (not dragging them into the sale), whilst also offering sufficient opportunity to finalise the deal. If your client has made a strong connection and is convinced by you, convert will happen. For some it will be simply a question of allowing them time to arrive at their decision; for others, however, you might just give that nudge to help. The skill you bring is to recognise when you need to do one or the other so that you keep the momentum going.

DITCHING THE HARD SELL

As we've seen, there's a big difference between a nudge and a push. Let's now look at why 'pushy' sales tactics don't work for gaining long-term, loyal clients. When your actions go way beyond a nudge and become a push, you're into 'hard sell' territory. We've all experienced the hard sell. Think of a New York tourist shop. The shop owner is standing outside, spruiking on the pavement. There are big,

[1] Frost, Aja, '60 Key Sales Statistics That'll Help You Sell Smarter in 2021', HubSpot, HubSpot, Inc., 8 January 2021, blog.hubspot.com/sales/sales-statistics

bold signs, announcing special offers and promotions, such as, 'FOR TODAY ONLY'.

The souvenir seller in New York (or any other tourist city for that matter) goes hard for the biggest single sale he or she can make because the chances are high that the customer isn't coming back. It's a one-off sale, not a long-term relationship with a loyal advocate. How often have you said to someone, 'If you're going to New York/London/Paris/Sydney, you simply *must* visit this great souvenir shop; they've got the best Empire State Building pencil sharpeners'. My bet is never. However, these sellers are not after the referral or the repeat sale; there's a high enough volume of new customers walking past their shop every day that they can operate on a policy of 'sell hard, sell once, move on'.

NO ONE LOVES ADS

'But wait', you say. 'I've used hard-sell strategies with clients before. Am I really as off-putting as a New York souvenir salesman?' In answer to that, I would like you to consider the following universal truth: no one likes being the recipient of a pushy 'hard sell'. Think of it this way: when you pick up a newspaper or magazine, how often do you turn straight to the ads? When you're watching TV, listening to a podcast, or seeing a movie at the cinema, do you look forward to watching products being promoted? I'd hazard a guess that the answer is overwhelmingly 'no'.

We read the newspaper for the articles and information within. We watch television, listen to podcasts, and go to the movies for entertainment and insight. The ads are often background noise, something to be endured, and where possible, skipped.

Just as we don't want to watch or listen to ads, neither do our prospective customers. We are more likely to convert, encouraging our clients to take the next step with us, if we provide genuinely useful information. If we can teach them something about a topic, share our informed opinions, or provide leadership expertise, we will engage with our audience. This approach, not a hard sell, is far more effective in getting them to take the next step, whether that is buying for the first time, buying again, or encouraging someone else to buy.

DON'T SHOUT

Closely linked to the hard sell is the 'shout' sell. When we're trying to convert, it's easy to believe that 'he who shouts the loudest wins'.

Sometimes the shouting is literal—have you noticed how many ads on TV, radio, and podcasts are now delivered at a volume that is louder than the program they interrupt? In written formats, 'shouting' often takes the form of leading with superlatives, such as, 'THE BIGGEST', 'THE BEST EVER', or 'THE LOWEST PRICE THIS YEAR'. Think of all those ads and websites where the first thing you see or hear is 'SALE!' or 'SPECIAL OFFER! ONE WEEK ONLY!'

Certainly, these ads are attention grabbing, but are they effective? I don't know about you, but I switch off quickly when I hear or see loud messages. I don't want to be shouted at. I find it rude, insulting to my intelligence, and downright annoying.

For me, shouted messages bring to mind images of the Army, where drill sergeants shout orders that demand blind obedience. One could argue that it is justifiable in that environment, but when we communicate a message about our company, product, or service, our goal is to win people over, not to insist that they follow orders with military precision. In civilian life, authority is far more effectively conveyed with a calm tone that communicates confidence, knowledge, and integrity.

The best example I have ever seen of the quiet, authoritative voice wasn't in the business world, but in the unruly atmosphere of a preschool classroom. My son's kinder teacher was a shining example of the art of serene authority. When the children arrived, they spent the first ten minutes running around and letting off steam before being called to sit down for the start of the class. Anyone wanting to be heard by two dozen four-year-olds might assume they would need to shout—but not Miss Jones. In a calm, authoritative voice, she would announce, 'Time to sit down, children', and the students instantly gave her their attention. Her message cut through the children's shouts and squeals like a knife through butter and was instantly heard (and obeyed).

As tempting as it may be to think that shouting is the fastest way to convert, Miss Jones shows us that the opposite is often true. A level-headed message delivered with integrity and authority is a much more powerful tool for conversion.

As a provider of a high-quality technology solution that solves client problems, you are looking for loyal advocates. You want long-term engagement with customers who will stay with you, bring in repeat revenue, and act as your best sales rep. You won't attract those people by shouting at them. The hard sell is therefore not an effective strategy for reaching your goals. In fact, over half (57%) of buyers say they'd be more likely to buy from someone who doesn't pressure them.[2] You may have done everything right to connect and convince, but if in the final step you simply shout at your prospects, you'll undo all that previous good work.

WHAT DOES A PUSH LOOK LIKE?

A push—or hard sell—is something that puts the client under pressure. It might be a deadline, such as, 'Buy now! This price is only available today/this week/to the end of the month!' Most frequently, it takes the form of discounts, by which I mean a 'something for nothing' discount, where you simply drop the price to get the sale. This is probably the least effective convert tactic possible if you want to generate long-term repeat clients. At best, giving away something for nothing sends the message that you're desperate. Desperation brings with it a whole host of other implications. For instance, it suggests that your product isn't as good as you say it is, and no one else wants to buy it. It can even imply that you were overcharging with your initial offer. This kind of

In the conversion process, the goal of each step is not necessarily to close the deal; often, it is simply to get to the next step. It might be scheduling the next meeting with a decision maker; it might be arranging a demonstration or proof of concept; it might even be as simple as the prospect subscribing to your newsletter so that you can continue your messaging.

dishonesty undoes all that great work you did to convince them that you were the right company for them. What does it say about what you think of your product and its value if you can simply reduce the price at the drop of a hat? Think back to what we said about congruence in Chapter 7—if you believe in your product and have convinced your prospect to believe in it as well, you are showing a lack of consistency if you then reduce its worth by reducing its price.

The 'something for nothing' discount is a different kettle of fish than 'tailoring'. If your offer is truly outside of the client's budget, and you can take something out in order to create a lower priced solu-

[2] Frost, Aja. '60 Key Sales Statistics That'll Help You Sell Smarter in 2021.' HubSpot. HubSpot, Inc., 8 January 2021. blog.hubspot.com/sales/sales-statistics.

tion, you are showing flexibility by tweaking your solution to their exact needs. This falls into 'nudge' territory, and it doesn't constitute a 'push'.

A push persuades the prospective client to do something they're not sure about, and afterwards they may regret their decision. This experience of 'buyer's remorse' may occur after a push, but it rarely happens after a nudge.

Consider also your integrity as a seller. A push puts you in a position in which you may lose leverage with your prospective clients. For example, if a discount is 'only until the end of the month', your customers who missed out on the sale may try to haggle with you when you raise your price on the first day of the next month.

CAN A PUSH WORK?

You might have found that reducing your price, adding a special incentive, or sending out an offer of 'Best Deal of the Year! Buy Now!' has worked in the past. You are correct, it does—with certain groups of buyers. However, are these the buyers you really want to attract? If you have to use hard sell tactics repeatedly to get sales, it's likely you're not cultivating long-term, loyal clients. Instead, these clients are more likely to be 'ship jumpers' who will go with you whilst you have an offer, then switch allegiances once someone else beats it. They may buy, but they don't do so because of you; they do it because of your immediate offer. That doesn't make for the repeat business that is at the very heart of the meaning of 'Convert'.

For example, one of my favourite business networking groups, Fresh Networking, exemplifies how to generate referral business through building relationships. They understand this notion of ditching the hard sell, and they incorporate it into the heart of their business model with their motto: 'If you sell, you will repel'.

Story

I often enjoy a bit of thrift shopping—I love discovering vintage items that I wouldn't find in regular stores. However, I have stopped going to my local charity shop because the salesperson there is so pushy. As soon as I pick something up, she will ask me, 'Do you like that? I can do it for half the ticket price'. Much of the pleasure in thrifting comes from browsing, so when I feel pressurised to buy, my enjoyment evaporates. I'd rather go somewhere else where I know that I will be left alone to peruse. When the shop owner gives me space, I'm far more likely to purchase something.

WHEN PUSH FEELS LIKE THE ONLY OPTION

If you're struggling to convert, and you feel like the hard sell is the only option you have, this is usually a sign that you've skipped too fast through an earlier part of the process—either strategy, connect, or convince.

Strategy

Have you developed a sufficiently detailed profile of your target audience? If you haven't, you might find it difficult to convert because you are not targeting the ideal buyer for your product or service. There is a customer for every price point, so if you feel that you have to offer a discount to win every deal, it could indicate that you have misidentified your target audience. The solution in this case is to return to Chapter 4 and strategically re-evaluate who your target audience is. If you have attracted the 'wrong' audience, the most important thing is to recognise this fact as early as possible and save the time and effort in trying to convert.

Let's return to our dating analogy from earlier in this chapter—in this scenario, the relationship is going well, and the couple is about to get an apartment together. It's only at this point that they realise that one person wants to live in New York and the other dreams of living in London. There's no compromise to be found. They are not each other's 'ideal audience' after all. Whilst I'm not suggesting this would have been a topic for discussion on the first date, it is an important part of the 'qualification' process.

A while back, I was approached by an agency for some writing work. I had been recommended to them, and they knew I offered what they wanted. However, when I gave them a quote, they immediately said that I was beyond their budget. I thanked them for the opportunity and agreed that my offer was not suitable for their requirement. I asked them to bear me in mind if they had other clients who were looking for what I did and had a budget to match. I didn't use hard sell tactics to get them to engage, nor did I lower my prices to court their business. No time was wasted on either side, and a door was still open for future opportunity.

Connect

Have you connected with your ideal customer? If you have correctly identified your target audience, but you are still struggling to communicate your offer, you might not have created a strong enough connection. If this is the case, review your communication and check it against the tips in Chapter 6. For example, are you using the right language to attract your target audience? If you want to attract people who are interested in your value, but your website hits visitors with special offers on your home page, you can't blame them if they think you're a business that will haggle and continue to reduce prices if they hold back from making a decision.

Convince

Have you given your ideal customer enough information to make them feel confident in your solution? If you have identified and connected with your target audience, but they are giving you price objections, you might not have spent enough time 'convincing' them of the benefits of your offer. If this is the case, return to Chapter 7 and review the strategies for creating communication that convinces. Rather than getting frustrated and making them a 'now or never' offer, keep the channels of communication open and redouble your efforts with your 'Convince' messaging. Your customer may just need a little more marinating before they are ready to convert.

Everyone Can Be Sold—You Can't Sell Everyone

You will never close every deal, and that's okay. No business has a 100% conversion rate. In fact, the Connect, Convince, Convert process helps you screen out prospective customers that are not a good fit. The earlier you identify the prospects who are not a good match, the better. This should ideally happen at the strategy stage, or during Connect or Convince.

In my corporate career, we were assigned a 'patch', or a number of organisations in a given industry who were our target clients. I remember one organisation in particular. I spent several weeks attending meetings with them before I realised that they were simply so far from our ideal client that they were never going to do business with us. It wasn't that they weren't a successful company; nor were their goals outside of our area of expertise. But whilst we had a process-driven approach with a 'do it once, do it right' mentality, they were a 'move fast, break things' organisation. Despite our respective successes, we were not the right company for them, and they were not the right client for us. Our disparate business philosophies were never going to meet in the middle.

Everyone is an ideal client for someone, but they're not necessarily the right client for you. The 'Connect' and 'Convince' stages of the process act as a filter for both you and your prospects, which significantly increases your conversion rate.

MAPPING THE STEPS

You've stoked up the furnace of conversion, your audience is convinced of your offer, and they're ready to act. But...they don't know what to do next. If you reduce your momentum at this point and leave your audience waiting for instructions, they will feel frustrated and confused. Despite all your hard work, you may still lose the sale. If your communication is to be effective at converting, it must provide your audience with a clear map of the next steps in the customer journey.

Just as with the stepping stones analogy in Chapter 2, there may be more than one possible route that your audience can take. There could be multiple paths to the sale, and the best one will depend on each individual client. Part of developing a customer profile is to determine how comfortable they are with your message, how quickly they are convinced, and how fast they are willing to move. For this reason, you will usually need more than one option, ensuring that there is always that 'shortcut' path for those who are willing to move straight to the purchase.

The key to conversion is to have no 'orphan communications'—that is, no message formats that leave the audience thinking, 'Yes, that makes sense, that sounds like what I need, but what do I do next?' There should never be a blockage along their route, and they should never feel stranded. Every piece of communication must clearly signpost the subsequent steps your prospect should take along their path to doing business with you.

I use the plural 'calls to action' deliberately — when you give your audience different options, you increase the 'convert power' of your message. Conversion is not a 'one size fits all' exercise; some of your audience will be ready to make a big leap to the next stone, whilst others will feel more comfortable with a smaller, easier step.

In Chapter 6, I talked about a VA who helped consultants in Melbourne with newsletters. I was impressed with her specificity, and it was enough to make me connect with her. However, am I doing business with her now? No, I'm not. Although I connected with her and indicated my interest, she didn't respond. She gave me no next step.

There is no shortage of options for next steps—most of the ten forms of communication play a part here, along with face-to-face meetings, calls, and demonstrations. Have your next stepping stone ready—once your prospect has read a case study, for example, give them a link to sign up to your newsletter. Your newsletter might prompt them to read your eBook, which could lead to them requesting an ROI model or an onsite trial.

Be prepared for each of these steps, knowing what you will offer the client and what your follow-up will be after each step. Together, these stepping stones create a path that your prospect can follow to get to the end goal.

MAKE CALLS TO ACTION

Having the next stepping stone ready with no dead ends means that you need calls to action. In its simplest form, a call to action is a targeted request. One party asks another party to accomplish a specific deed that is in the interests of both.

Let's revisit our dating analogy. Our couple is on their first date, and they are getting on well, taking small steps. However, they are on a path to nowhere if at the end of the evening they don't ask for the next step—a phone number, another date. So, whilst they are right to avoid skipping too many milestones and jumping straight to the endgame, they still need to keep the momentum of their relationship going.

As a provider of a high-quality technology solution that solves client problems, you are looking for loyal advocates. You want long-term engagement with customers who will stay with you, bring in repeat revenue, and act as your best sales rep. You won't attract those people by shouting at them. The hard sell is therefore not an effective strategy for reaching your goals.

I use the plural 'calls to action' deliberately—when you give your audience different options, you increase the 'convert power' of your message. Conversion is not a 'one size fits all' exercise; some of your audience will be ready to make a big leap to the next stone, whilst others will feel more comfortable with a smaller, easier step.

For example, you may place a call to action on your website, encouraging your prospects to contact you for more information, which caters to those who are ready to take a bigger stride and engage directly. Your website may also include some 'find out more' calls to action to keep prospects on your site for longer, or a 'download the eBook' call to action that keeps you uppermost in their mind as an expert and potential advisor.

For those ready to leap, you may want to include a 'buy now' call to action, but if this is the only option that you provide your prospects, you risk moving into hard sell territory.

THE PURPOSE OF CALLS TO ACTION

Calls to action perform an essential role in conversion—your prospects won't know what you are asking them to do unless you state it clearly. Think about the person with whom you are communicating and consider what you want them to do at each step. Then ask them to do it.

The language you use in your call to action can have a significant influence on whether it is followed. This language can be hard to get right. It requires you to be compelling without being aggressive, friendly without being weak, and engaging without being corny.

There are many ways to write calls to action. Some of the most effective include:

- → Expressing benefits:
  - Learn more about the benefits of…
  - To explore how you could reduce your costs, talk to our industry specialists.
- → Urging directly:
  - Let's get started.
  - Learn more.
  - Let's start the discussion.
- → Encouraging immediate action:
  - Give us a call today.
  - Get in touch now.
- → Expressing interest:
  - We're keen to learn more about your business.
  - We'd love to discuss your next project. Give us a call.
- → Using the customer's words:
  - I'm interested, please send me more information.
  - I'm in—book me a place now.

→　Employing active verbs:
- Start your journey.
- Find the solution that works for your business.

All too often we risk falling at the last hurdle because we don't use our communication to ask clearly for what we want. A good call to action allows you to reach the finish line so both you and your customer can win the race.

BE PRECISE

The more precise you are about what you are asking someone to do, the more likely they are to do it. So, when you are building your calls to action, aim to be as direct as possible. Vague instructions are far less likely to be followed.

The biggest culprit for vague language is 'If', as in, 'If you want more information...' Indecisive words like 'if' automatically introduce an element of doubt.

When it comes to calls to action, I recommend the 'toddler technique'. Of course, I'm not advocating that you treat your clients like children; this strategy refers to keeping your communication specific, clear, and concise. The rationale is this—anyone who has interacted with a toddler knows that if you give them a generalised task, you don't get very far. If you ask your toddler, 'Get ready to go to grandma's house', they are far less likely to act than if you say, 'Please put on your blue shoes now'. The specific action ('put on your shoes'), with a qualifier ('the blue ones') and a timeframe ('now') gives them a much more tangible instruction to follow.

It's not really any different with adults, whether in social or business situations. We all know that the rather vague 'Keep in touch' is what we say when we don't actually mean it. When we want to keep in touch, we say, 'I'll call you on Tuesday' or 'Are you free on Friday for a coffee?'

Therefore, an effective call to action requires us to be specific, clear, and concise.

Specific

Our audience, just like a toddler, needs to understand what it is we want them to do. No doubt, no 'ifs'—just a specific direction. Being specific in your call to action might include:
- →　What to do: Visit our website to subscribe to our newsletter.
- →　What to expect: You'll receive a newsletter once a month.

→ When to complete the action: Subscribe before the 6th of the month to receive our current newsletter.
→ Who to contact: Contact our team for more details.
→ Where to go: Follow the link to our subscription page.

Clear

The call to action should not be open to interpretation. If you tell a toddler, 'Get ready for a playdate with Jack', they might interpret your words as 'Gather all your favourite toys and put them into a bag'. If what you mean by 'Get ready' is 'Put on your brown jumper and your blue runners', then that is what you must say to get that result. In the same way, when you are communicating through an indirect medium like a website or an eBook, your message must be clear and lead directly to the outcome you want.

Concise

If you give a toddler a list of five tasks to do, they will feel overwhelmed, and few of their assignments will get done. Keep it short and sweet. Toddlers don't have subtlety in their communication yet—the language we use with them is a relatively blunt instrument. However, that doesn't mean we should be patronising or talk down to them. Toddlers may not have a sophisticated lexicon, but they do have an excellent nose for sniffing out manipulation. Similarly, when you engage with customers, you must communicate with both precision and empathy to achieve your goal.

BE PERSONAL

Communication is personal, so make your call to action personal. With a call to action, you're often talking through an impersonal medium, such as a website, article, or eBook. Wherever possible, use the client's name, either as an individual or a business, or refer specifically to their industry.

You can also make a personal connection through your staff. When it comes to introducing your people, use names and photos where you can. Photos and bios offer a personal touch for non-personal communications. For example, I have a client who uses the personal touch to great effect on their website—as you look through their products, you see the name, photo, and phone number of the person to call for more information. Below each product set is a call to action that invites you, for instance, to 'Call Scott now to discuss your requirements'.

MAKE IT EASY

When you're mapping out the steps of your call to action, make it as easy as possible for your prospects to follow those steps. It could be as simple as emphasising a link that will allow them to download your eBook, highlighting an FAQ page on your website, or training your customer service staff to answer their questions, rather than giving them a vague, 'I'll get someone to call you back'.

As an example of the latter, a contact of mine who runs an SEO business helped a leading university discover that they were failing to convert some great leads. Their call to action was asking prospective clients to ring, but those calls were going to people who didn't know about the campaign or the service it was promoting. The university was doing a great job of connecting and convincing, but they failed to convert by making the process too hard.

Likewise, if you offer online chat, be aware that it can be a double-edged sword. If it can provide genuinely useful, personalised information and answers to specific questions, it can help move your prospective customer through your 'stepping stone' process. However, automated chat systems that give stock answers can have the opposite effect, frustrating your visitors and turning them away.

The language you use in your call to action can have a significant influence on whether it is followed. This language can be hard to get right. It requires you to be compelling without being aggressive, friendly without being weak, and engaging without being corny.

If your website offers the chance to buy there and then, make it simple. Think about the messages that could be implicit in the way that you ask your customers to engage. For example, if part of your value proposition is that your product is easy to use, but your website's checkout page confuses your audience (unclear purchasing information, vague pricing or delivery costs, or too many clicks to checkout, just to list a few examples), you might be undermining your whole message.

CAROL BENTON

FOCUSSING ON THE BENEFITS

Throughout this book, I have returned several times to a discussion of benefits—and with good reason. Remember, customers buy the outcome of your solution. Your clients don't want your products and features—they want what your products and features can do for them. When you focus on benefits, you reduce buyer's remorse and increase customer satisfaction. Conversion that is centred around benefits creates happy clients who are ready and willing to transact. These clients come back to you time and again, and they tell others about the fantastic benefits of working with you.

TELL A BENEFITS STORY

Storytelling is the most powerful form of communication—it draws the audience in, engages them, and builds a relationship with the key players. So, as you focus on the benefits, aim to tell a story—a story where the customer is the hero. Describe how they will overcome their challenges, achieve their goals and aspirations, and reap the rewards of working with you. The benefits story allows you to pull together everything you have told them so far and weave it into a compelling narrative with them at the centre.

Think of the old adage about buying the hole, not the drill bit—no one buys a drill bit for its features alone. They buy it because it's going to help them quickly create a hole that is the right size for their project. So, if we're to convert, we have to tell the story of the hole, not the drill bit.

BENEFITS ARE THE ULTIMATE 'CONVERSION' TOOL

Benefits are the way in which your prospective client's business will change as a result of engaging with you and your product or solution. Once you focus on the customer and the difference that you can make for them, conversion happens much more smoothly.

I worked with a client who wanted to make her proposals more engaging. She knew that this would strengthen her ability to convert. A review of her past proposals showed that she was consistently outlining her offer and her price; however, the last link in the chain was missing. She wasn't communicating the benefits of her solution. She understood the benefits that her clients would enjoy, and she assumed that they did too. It's possible that some of them did, but rather than assume, we modified her proposal format to include a section clearly titled 'Benefits', and we listed in bullet point format all the ways in which her clients would profit from working with her.

Clearly articulated benefits can also lead to referrals. If you've got a delighted client who wants to tell someone else about you, the best endorsement they can give is one which describes how you've helped them. Benefits are the story that your clients tell other prospective clients, such as, 'You should talk to "XYZ" company; they really helped me to save on production costs/grow my market share/ improve customer satisfaction scores'.

BENEFITS ARE INDIVIDUAL

In Chapter 4, we looked at the fact that 'benefits are in the eye of the beholder'—they vary for each potential customer or group of customers. As you develop your strategy, conduct research to determine which benefits your target audience values and focus your communication to articulate how you provide these benefits.

Benefits might include:
→ Increased revenue
→ Cost savings
→ Company peace of mind
→ Compliance with regulations
→ Consumer engagement and satisfaction

The key is to examine the full range of benefits that apply to your client. You can analyse the benefits of your solution by asking 'So What' to check whether you are describing a genuine customer benefit or just another feature. Go back to your client's aspirations and objectives. Explain to them how you will help them overcome the hurdles that stand between them and their aspirations and describe how you will work with them to reach their goals.

Helping someone to accomplish their dream or goal is incredibly powerful. Imagine the thing that you would most like to achieve in the world. Think about what it would be like to reach that goal—to feel that sense of attainment, satisfaction, and completion. Then imagine that someone tells you how they can help you to get there. You know this person, you've made a connection, you trust them, and you believe them. They can help you achieve your ultimate dream. How much more convincing to you need? None, I suspect—you'd be ready to sign up with them there and then.

Story

When I was younger, I had always wanted to run a marathon, but as a short distance 'jogger', I didn't think I would ever be able to manage it. I joined a running club, and the coach convinced me that with the help of his training program, I could run the 42 km. I followed his instructions to the letter, and to my amazement, I completed the race. The power in his message came from him articulating how he could help me achieve a dream. I am not only still a member of that running club, but I have also told dozens of other people how great I think it is.

So, the most powerful tool possible with conversion is to show your audience how you will move them towards that goal or aspiration. If your audience understands how your product or service will move them forward, they will buy from you again and refer you to others. That is true conversion.

Communicating to Convert

Just as you did in Chapters 6 and 7, take a few moments to review your 'Convert' communications against the tips above.

Do you have any 'orphan communications'—those that leave the reader hanging, unsure of where to go next?

Do your communications use a hard sell, rather than a nudge?

Are you making multiple calls to action? Are they precise, personalised, and easy?

Are you focussing on the benefits and helping the customer 'join the dots' of your solution?

Use the table below to note anything in your communication that needs some more work, using a yes/no, a 1–5, or a high/medium/low ranking.

WORKSHEET: YOUR TURN

	TAKE YOUR TIME	GIVE THEM A NUDGE	NO HARD SELL	CALLS TO ACTION	FOCUS ON THE BENEFITS
Website					
Articles					
Presentations					
Case Studies					
eBooks					
Newsletter					
Proposal					

Revisit Strategy, Connect, and Convince

If you're finding conversion difficult, evaluate where the root cause might be. Review the above section, 'When Push Feels Like the Only Option', to check whether you need to revisit your strategy, your 'Connect', and/or your 'Convince' stages.

NOTES

NEXT STEPS

Now that we've looked at the key tips for ensuring that our communication connects, convinces, and converts, we're going to continue with the theme of practical implementation. In the next chapter, we will take a more in-depth look at the ways in which you can structure your ten communication formats. This analysis will give you a strong framework and starting point for your communication to which you can then apply the tips we've just explored. To use an analogy, these structures of communication are like a Christmas tree, and the tips we've been learning are like the decorations we get to hang on it. We've got a box full of decorations, so next we're going to find the perfect tree to display them.

CAROL BENTON

CHAPTER 9

Practical Applications of Connect, Convince, Convert

LET'S RECAP

As we've progressed through our exploration of Connect, Convince, Convert, we've gone from the theory to creating a strategy. We've reviewed the 10 Forms of Business Communication. We've learnt tips and techniques to ensure that our communication does its job at each stage of the customer journey. In this chapter, we will look at practical ways to apply those structures.

Every form of business communication has a structure. A structure gives our communication shape and support. It forms the base to which we apply our words and images. To echo the analogy from Chapter 8, think of a Christmas tree. If our words are the decorations, the structure is the Christmas tree on which we hang them. If we start with a good, strong, beautifully shaped tree, our decorations will have a bigger impact—they will say 'It's Christmas' far more effectively.

'RECIPES' FOR BUSINESS COMMUNICATION

When my kids were young, part of their birthday ritual was choosing the cake they wanted me to make for them. Like millions of other mothers in Australia, the *Women's Weekly Kids' Birthday Cakes* book was my bible. It not only had beautiful pictures of a pirate ship, an alien, a castle, and other fun cake designs for my children to choose from, but it also provided detailed instructions for me to follow, including templates tucked in the back of the book to help cut the cakes to the right shape. Think of this chapter as the instructions and the templates. If you follow these recipes, you will create some delectable pieces of business communication.

I am going to share with you some structural outlines, or templates, for each of the ten forms of communication that we discussed in Chapter 5. I am not saying that these are the only structures you could use; however, starting with a structure is more efficient and effective than starting with a blank screen. When you're creating a piece of communication, the structure speeds up the process by giving you a clear framework, allowing you to 'fill in the blanks'.

These structures ensure that each piece of communication does its designated job, taking your audience on the Connect, Convince, Convert journey.

1: ELEVATOR PITCH

As we saw in Chapter 5, the elevator pitch is an invaluable tool for opening the door to opportunity. At the same time, it is a communication format that even experienced businesspeople struggle to master. I have seen sales reps, business owners, and CEOs, all of whom possessed a strong message in their company's written material, fail to express their value proposition succinctly in verbal form.

Whether it's a formal introduction in a business meeting or a 'what do you do' moment at a barbecue, the elevator pitch is often your first chance to connect, and the words you say will impact the future of that connection. So, it is worth spending some time planning your response and having something ready to say.

There are two versions of the elevator pitch: the 1-minute pitch and the 10-second intro. The structure I recommend for the 1-minute pitch has three parts—the Introduction, the Expansion, and the Close. Embedded within this structure you also have your 10-second intro. So, once you have your 1-minute pitch mastered, you will have the elements of the shorter version as well.

Here is the structure of the elevator pitch at a glance:
→ Part 1: The Introduction
   • Name
   • Category
   • Value
→ Part 2: The Expansion
   • Problem/Solution/Outcome
     OR
   • Customer Story
     OR
   • Step-By-step
→ Part 3: The Close
   • The Ask

1) THE INTRODUCTION

The first part of your elevator pitch covers the basics: name, category, and value.

Name

'That's easy', you may be thinking, 'I know how to say my name.' Of course you do, but there are a few additional things to consider when using your name in a pitch. Are you in a social or business setting? How well do you know the person you're talking to? Depending on these factors, the way you introduce yourself by name might vary. You might simply use your given name (first name only, or first and last), or you might also include the name of your business.

Do also be aware that we are so used to saying our own name that we can inadvertently rush, mumble, or garble it. Remember that an elevator pitch is a verbal form of communication—your audience has no visual clues (no slides, no written documents), so unless you speak clearly, your listeners will not decipher, let alone remember, your name.

Rushing or mumbling your name also risks giving your audience the message, 'This is not important'. So, slow down, articulate your name and your company name clearly, and give it the weight and importance it deserves.

Category

This is the category you and/or your business fall into. Categories are useful shorthand for the listener, so that they instantly understand at a general level what you do. If you're in a recognised profession, this is simple (e.g. 'I'm a software developer', or 'I'm a lawyer'). If your role is more generic (for example, a sales manager), you might want to add the type of company. (E.g. 'I'm a sales leader with a technology distributor'.) This 'sets the scene' for your audience.

Value

This is where you talk about who you help and how you help them. It's the part of the elevator pitch that sets you apart from the others in your category. Value is arguably the most important aspect of your introduction, but it is the part that is most often left out.

Value consists of who you help, what you do for them, and the outcome you help them achieve. It's a tall order to condense this into one or two sentences, but it can certainly be done.

The structure here is:

'I help / work with **[category of person or business — i.e. your identified target audience]** to **[outcome or benefit]** by **[solution]**'.

For example,

'I help **technology companies** to **win more business** by **clearly articulating their value**'.

2) THE EXPANSION

If Part 1 captures your audience's attention, Part 2 gives them a little more detail to forge the connection. There are several ways you can do this.

Problem/Solution/Outcome

You can expand on the problem, solution, and outcome. Essentially, you take the 'I help…' statement from your introduction and give a bit more detail. For example:

→ 'Many technology companies are great at what they do, but they struggle to put it into words for effective communication. I help them define a clear message strategy and then implement it consistently through a twelve-month program. The result is that they connect with their audience, convince them to engage, and convert them to take action, leading to more business, with customers who are loyal advocates.'

Customer Story

You can describe how you helped one of your clients. Stories are often the best way to illustrate what you do and the outcomes you've achieved for others. Names, facts, and statistics will bring the story to life. For example:

→ 'I have been working with [ABC Company], a software developer who wanted to expand into new markets. I facilitated a strategy workshop to draw out their key value message. Then we reviewed their current communication, revised it to consistently reflect their message, and created new forms of content to reach their new audience. They have seen engagement and leads grow by 20% over the last year.'

Step-By-Step

You can take the listener through a 'step-by-step' description of your solution. For example:

→ 'I take companies through a three-step system: Firstly, we go through a communication strategy process to articulate their key messages. Then we create or refresh their written forms of communication, such as their website, brochures, LinkedIn profiles, and articles. Finally, we train their teams to deliver the same consistent message verbally.'

3) THE CLOSE

This is where you sum up and/or ask for something. Remember from Chapter 8 that we want no orphan communications, so don't leave your listener hanging with no next steps to follow.

The Ask

Your ask can be short and simple, for example:
- → 'If you know someone who would like to communicate more effectively, let's have a coffee.'
- → 'I'm looking for introductions to technology companies who'd like to win more business. Please ask them to get in touch to discuss how I can help.'

THE 10-SECOND INTRO

The good news is that once you've created your 1-minute pitch, you also have your 10-second intro.

You simply take the Category and Value parts of your intro, and you've got the answer to 'What do you do?'. This is exactly what I did in the situation I described in Chapter 5, where my 10-second intro (given in response to a surgeon asking, 'What do you do?') led to me gaining a new client.

The three parts described above will produce a great elevator pitch that will open doors. If you want to take it up yet another notch, there are a couple of variations you might want to try.

THE 'RELATABLE STATEMENT' VARIATION

This is a variation on the 1-minute pitch, which aims to get instant engagement by starting with the problem or the aspiration. The Relatable Statement comes immediately before your introduction, and it draws your audience in before you even state your name. For example:
- → Start with a 'You know how…' or 'Do you ever…' question to highlight the problem.
- → Lead with an 'Imagine if' statement to get the listener to dream about their aspiration.
- → Make a bold statement to set the scene, such as, 'Technology transforms business and changes lives'.

THE 'SUPERHERO' VARIATION

Some people are confident enough to use a Superhero Name or an Unexpected Category for their business.

Examples of Superhero Names include:

→ The Shift Initiator
→ The Abundance Activator
→ The Numbers Whisperer
→ His Royal Freshness

Examples of Unexpected Categories I have heard are:

→ 'I make grown men cry' (a grief counsellor for fathers who have lost a child).
→ 'I'm a death walker' (a counsellor who works with the terminally ill).

It's interesting to note that both these examples are of serious, sombre businesses, but Unexpected Categories can apply equally well to businesses with a lighter mission.

TRAPS TO AVOID IN THE ELEVATOR PITCH

1) Being Too Detailed or Long-Winded

When you know something well, it can be hard to leave stuff out, but that's exactly what you must do to create an effective elevator pitch. You must condense the important parts of your message into about sixty seconds. It is often the case that shorter forms of communication take longer to create. The French philosopher Pascal epitomised this when he stated, 'I would have written a shorter letter, but I did not have the time'.

When you only have seconds to communicate, every single word must be considered for its impact on your pitch. This is where it is helpful to ask yourself, 'So What?' If you can't decide which details to omit from your pitch, ask yourself 'So What' after each one to determine its relative importance to your target audience. Only include the top-level details that have passed this screening process.

2) Describing Your Role Instead of Your Value

If you work for a company, especially a corporate, it's easy to give your job title, rather than saying what you actually do. Many companies operate as hierarchies where your title and status are important internally. Whilst they may be important to you and your company, they may not connect with your listener. Instead, tell your listener about what you do and what value you add to your company's clients.

3) Lacking Clear Value

Some pitches are too generic. For example, 'We develop software' or 'We're a solution provider' don't tell your listener who you are or how you offer value.

4) Making It 'All About Me'

Like every other form of communication, the elevator pitch must focus on who and how you help. Some pitches fall into the trap of being a sixty-second bragging session, which won't form that sought after connection with the listener.

REPURPOSING THE ELEVATOR PITCH

When you complete your elevator pitch, you can repurpose it as your positioning statement. You may need to edit the language to reflect the formality of the written format, but the structure is the same. You can use this statement in an introductory email, in a brochure, in the catalogue for a trade show or exhibition, or as part of your speaker bio.

> **The first thing your visitors should see on your home page is themselves. This means that through the words and images you use, your prospective customers can see that you understand them, speak their language, and have something to offer them. Your content expresses their biggest issues, articulates their dreams, and describes how you can help them reach their goals.**

2: WEBSITE

When it comes to websites, there are as many layouts as there are sites. I am not suggesting here that there is a 'one size fits all' website for your business, nor am I offering any recommendations on the design of a site. There are many talented web developers to help you with that. That being said, I want you to be aware that there are key content elements that need to be present on your website for it to effectively engage your audience.

Think of these as the essential 'building blocks' of your site, which exist within its overall style and design. This section therefore doesn't give you a structure that you must follow; instead, it provides you with

'WHAT SHOULD I WRITE ABOUT?' IS A QUESTION THAT MANY OF MY CLIENTS ASK ME. MY ADVICE IS TO WRITE WHAT YOU KNOW. IT IS EASY TO UNDERESTIMATE THE VALUE OF YOUR INTELLECTUAL PROPERTY AND KNOWLEDGE, BUT THE CHANCES ARE THAT YOU HAVE INFORMATION THAT IS OF GENUINE VALUE TO YOUR TARGET AUDIENCE.

a checklist of the blocks of content that will make your site 'sticky' and engaging for your audience. You need to be sure that when your potential customer visits your site, they see all these elements, and that each element does its designated job—to connect, convince, or convert.

Compare your existing site against this checklist and see how you stack up. It may confirm that your site is doing a fabulous job, or it might show you a few areas that you could improve.

HOME PAGE

Think of your home page as a 'taster menu', giving small bites to show the flavour of what is in the rest of the site. A home page is about snippets—little blocks of information that build a quick connection and make the visitor want to stay and read more. The content building blocks for a home page are short but essential.

Overview of What You Offer

This is where you get to repurpose your elevator pitch, condensing it into a more succinct format. Essentially, it has to capture in a very few words what you do and how you help.

Customer Mirror

The first thing your visitors should see on your home page is themselves. This means that through the words and images you use, your prospective customers can see that you understand them, speak their language, and have something to offer them. Your content expresses their biggest issues, articulates their dreams, and describes how you can help them reach their goals. As they scan your home page, they will see something they need or want, and they will understand that you have shared values and a shared approach. That's a lot to do in a few seconds, but without this connection, your message will be just so much background party chatter.

It may well be that you have more than one target audience, in which case you need to separate your communications so that each message addresses a specific group. You can still address multiple audiences through a single website, so long as you ensure that each group can 'see themselves' and go straight to the appropriate part of the site. Images in the form of photos or icons can also help in this instance, as they did for the customer that I cited in Chapter 6 who had several target audiences.

Benefits

We know that customers buy benefits, so a good home page will always have a summary of how the visitor will benefit from what you offer. What will they get out of it? This could be in the form of words only, or you might use a short 'explainer' video that covers your offer. Images are very powerful, so a picture of someone enjoying the benefits of your solution can 'speak a thousand words'.

Testimonials

As we saw in Chapter 5, using the words of others is a powerful way to convince prospective customers about the merits of your solution, so it can be an important part of your marketing strategy to include short testimonial quotes on your home page. These aren't full case studies (those merit their own page); all you need is one or two sentences to show that you're not the only one who thinks you're great. If your quotes are taken from longer case studies that appear on another part of your site, consider giving visitors a 'read the full story' call to action, which links to the case study page.

If you have customers that are well-known in your target industry, you might simply include their logos, ideally with a link through to case studies.

Calls to Action

Don't forget to give customers multiple opportunities to engage, whether it's to stay on the site for longer (a 'read more' call to action) or to move to the next stage (a 'contact/call us/get in touch' call to action).

Credentials

Whilst the best credential is the words of others, you may want to include another form of credential, such as an award or certification. It's important that this takes a lower priority on the page than the 'customer-facing' elements. There are so many websites where the home page starts by touting the company's awards and accolades. Credentials are important, but it is pointless to tell your audience how great you are before they know whether you have what they need.

Subscription

A subscription is a form of call to action. You may want to invite customers to subscribe to receive more information from you. This is often done with a pop-up window. It can be an effective way to bring your newsletter to your visitors' attention, but think carefully about timing. I don't know about you, but I get frustrated when I've only been on a site for a few seconds, and I'm invited to sign up.

Home Page Checklist

The order and style of these elements will depend on the design of your particular website. That's why the above is not so much a 'structure', but rather a checklist to ensure that your home page has all the right elements to do its main job—that of connecting. Like an elevator pitch, a home page must convey a succinct message with relatively few words. So, every word must be carefully selected for its ability to create effective communication.

OTHER PAGES

The other pages included on your website will vary depending on the structure of your business and the identity of your target audience. Here are a few guidelines about how to get the most from your site.

About Page

The 'About' page is often where you make the emotional connection with your audience. This is where you can share your 'why', explain the passion behind what you do, and introduce people to your team.

You may also want to share the story of your business, but a word of caution. Many 'About' pages start with history—you know the ones: 'Founded in 19XX, ABC company first did this, then did that...' I liken this approach to meeting someone, asking what they do, and then getting their life story. Think back to our cocktail party from Chapter 4. What if your conversation partner started their introduction with, 'Well, I started my career in 1958 as a tea boy, then I worked my way up to the mail room...' You wouldn't stay interested for long, and you would be unlikely to build a rapport with them.

Imagine instead if they started with, 'I have always been driven by finding more efficient ways to do things, using technology to free up time and save money, so I work at ABC company where we help supply chain organisations to do just that'. That answer is both relevant and personal, which encourages building a connection.

Video and photos work well here, too, making the site visitor feel that they are 'meeting' you. I worked with a company that is known for its dynamic, engaging staff, so we created a 'Meet the Team' page. The page introduces the team members with a photo and a short, slightly quirky bio of each of their people.

Blog Page

Articles are a great way for your site to be found, especially if they answer your target audience's key questions. Since articles are an important asset on a site, I recommend giving them their own page, rather than 'burying' them in another page.

Curated content can be valuable too. It doesn't all have to be written by you, so long as you put your spin and value on it. The most important part of a blog is to post consistently. See Section 4 below for some easy ideas for articles and blogs.

Some sites have a page called 'News', but this can be problematic for two reasons:

→ If you are going to call something 'news', you have to commit to regular posting. If the last thing on your 'news' page was six months ago, you've instantly undermined your credibility.

→ Make sure it really is news—something that is of interest to your customer. I have seen plenty of 'news' items about the company attending a trade show, for instance. If you're going to talk about this kind of 'news', make sure you explain why it is important for your customers to know about it. 'News', like benefits, is in the eye of the beholder.

Case Studies

Whether you call it 'case studies', 'customers', or 'success stories', this is important content to have on your site. Like blogs and articles, however, case studies often get buried on a website. I recommend placing these stories on their own clearly named page.

HOME

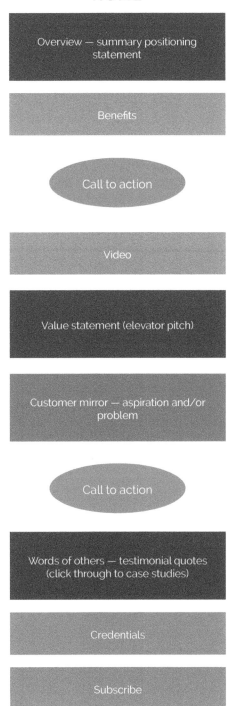

Overview — summary positioning statement

Benefits

Call to action

Video

Value statement (elevator pitch)

Customer mirror — aspiration and/or problem

Call to action

Words of others — testimonial quotes (click through to case studies)

Credentials

Subscribe

3: BROCHURE

A brochure acts as your proxy, something you can leave with the customer to remind them of you. Unlike an article or an eBook, a brochure can be more sales-oriented. The following structure ensures that your brochure will have a strong, clear message:

→   The Audience and Their Context
→   The Aspiration or Problem
→   The Solution
→   Benefits
→   Credentials
→   Call to action

These are the key building blocks that give a brochure the power to do its job. Now, let's take a look at how these content blocks can be applied to create a four-page brochure.

FRONT COVER

Let's analyse the brochure for my company, Words2Win, to see

how these elements go together to produce effective communication. The front cover starts with a punch, by introducing the company's benefits in the form of a succinct value statement. Not surprisingly, it looks similar to an elevator pitch. (Once again, we see the power of repurposing!)

The Audience and Their Context

Who are you talking to? What is their situation? As we learnt in Chapter 4 (Question 2), this information about your audience comes from your strategy. In this example, we see a short statement within the 'Communicate your value' section at the top of page 2, indicating that the brochure addresses companies who are strong at creating great tech.

The Aspiration or Problem

This is where you outline the problem you solve, using your clients' language. In this example, it is also contained in 'Communicate your value'. This takes up to 25% of the space—in this case, just under half a page.

The Solution

This is where you describe your product or service. Ideally, you'll break it down into three to five steps, points, or sub-offerings to make it easier to read and digest. Each of these points may also need to set the scene by describing the problem it solves. This takes the remainder of the middle two pages.

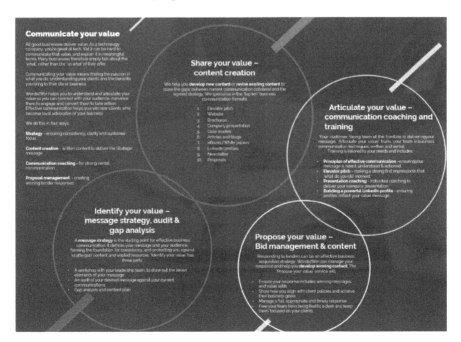

Benefits

This summary of outcomes can be stated directly, or it can be expressed through customer quotes, as in this example. If you use testimonials, choose a selection of one- or two-sentence quotes that highlight all the benefits you want to communicate. You need to include the name of the organisation and ideally the person and their role. A logo is good for capturing attention.

Credentials

What makes you good at what you do? To answer this question, return to the strategy in Chapter 4 (Question 4). You can also repurpose this information from the 'About' page on your website. In the example below, the credentials appear in the 'About' section at the top of page 4.

Call to Action

Include a call to action so that you don't leave your prospects hanging. Even a simple 'Get in touch' will do. Make sure to include your contact details.

Here's a final word if you are printing your brochures. The more professional the design, the heavier the paper, and the higher quality the finish, the better the brochure will convey authority and professionalism. All these factors make your brochure more likely to be kept, read, passed on, or actioned.

About Words2Win

Carol Benton, Director and founder, built the Words2Win program based on her experience of business communication – good and bad - in a 30-year career with technology powerhouses IBM and Toshiba. Carol created a wide range of business communications including proposals that won millions of dollars, and represented IBM in print and television media.

A languages degree honed her understanding of the power of effective communication and was enhanced by first class business training at:

- The London Business School
- Macquarie Graduate School of Management
- The Chartered Institute of Marketing

Carol has a skill for translation – quickly getting to the heart of even the most complex solutions, and representing them in the most appropriate form for the audience – to help Words2Win clients enhance their communications to win more business.

Carol's expertise is based on 30 years of international corporate sales, marketing and leadership, combined with industry-leading education.

Client Success

"The strategy workshop really clarified our value proposition and messaging"
Mike Mitchell, CEO, Neo Products

"Having the strategy in place meant that everything we did referred back to our key messages – we are 100% consistent in our communication."
Lawrence Pelletier, Sales and Marketing Director, Redcat

"Words2Win has helped us to elevate our executive content"
Mia Farber – VP Marketing, CitiXSys

"We engaged Words2Win to manage an RFP response, which was an important factor in us winning the tender"
Evan Thomas, Networking and Healthcare Division Manager, Sektor Distributors

"We now have a website which has generated leads for our business"
Scott Munro, Owner, FutureNet

"Words2Win shapes a proposal response that clearly answers each question and articulates our value."
Justin Lowe, Executive Director, ASI

"There is no better way to explain how we help our clients than to tell their stories. I had a very positive response to the case studies Words2Win developed."
Doron Rom, Managing Director, IMI

"Words2Win ran a workshop that captured what drives us, who we help, what we offer them and the difference it makes."
Catriona Byrne, Creative Director, Risesmart Australia

Get in touch

To talk about how you could win more business with a strategic message, engaging content, first class communication skills and winning proposals, contact Words2Win:

carolbenton@words2win.com.au
+ 61 431 671879
www.words2win.com.au

4: ARTICLES AND BLOGS

Sharing useful information builds tremendous credibility. Everyone wants to engage with people who know what they're talking about. If you share your insights and experience, your audience will see you as an expert. Rest assured that you don't have to be the world authority on a topic to add value—from your customer's perspective, 'expert' means someone who knows more about a topic than they do. We all naturally prefer to buy from someone who understands the problem we face and can articulate the solution, so by showing yourself to be a specialist in your topic, you enhance your connection and credibility.

STRUCTURE

Articles come in all forms and lengths, but 500 to 700 words is a sweet spot to aim for. This word count is short enough to engage most readers, yet long enough for you to make your point.

The structure of an article can be broken into three main parts:

→ **Intro**: This part sets the scene for the problem you are going to solve. It makes a relatable statement to draw the audience in.

→ **Body:** This part contains your main arguments and the information you want to share.

→ **Close:** This part is a summary that resolves the problem posed in the intro, and it includes a call to action.

Within the body of the article, there is a wide range of structures you can use to present your information. The structure you pick will depend on the style of your article, so choose a structure that is most appropriate to your message. The examples below will give you some ideas to get you started.

1) Numbered List

This is a popular format used on many blogs. For example, '9 ways to make your customers love you' or '5 reasons your developers lose productivity'. It's popular because it works—readers love list articles, and the structure makes these articles easy to write.

2) Pendulum

In this format, you describe alternate approaches to an issue and arrive at a preferred one or a compromise. For example, 'On the one hand, there's approach A, and on the other hand, approach B. The ideal is approach C.'

3) Question and Answer

In this format, you pose the questions that customers most frequently ask, and you answer them in the paragraphs of the article. This can also be a variation on the numbered list, e.g. 'The three most common questions about barcode printers'.

4) Concentric Circles

This format allows you to work your way from the outside in—or vice versa—typically in three steps. Examples of these 'concentric circles' could include:

→ **Geography:** how a particular issue impacts London, the UK, and the world.
→ **Market:** the benefits of a particular approach for the client's internal team, their customers, and their shareholders.

5) Timeline

This is a straightforward approach where you look at the past, present, and future. This format adapts well to technology, where things change rapidly. For example, you could describe what life was like before a particular solution was launched, the difference it's making now, and where it could lead in the future.

6) Mnemonic or Alliteration

In this format, you can take a word that is relevant to your topic and use the letters to illustrate the key points you want to make. Given that the world of tech loves acronyms, this slightly quirky approach often works well. A variation on this format is to use alliteration, such as 'The three Cs of customer service'.

TOPICS

Of course, there's more to creating an effective article than choosing the right structure. The biggest hurdle many people have when writing articles is selecting a topic. 'What should I write about?' is a question that many of my clients ask me. My advice is to write what you know. It is easy to underestimate the value of your intellectual property and knowledge, but the chances are that you have information that is of genuine value to your target audience. This may be knowledge that you take for granted—for example, when you understand a topic well, it can sometimes be hard to realise that others don't have the same understanding as you.

The thing about 'common knowledge' is that it is not as common as you think. If you're in the business of selling printers, for example, you might think that everyone understands the difference between various print technologies and knows which are best for a given situation. However, many of your prospective customers don't have this level of expertise in what, after all, is your specialist area.

I worked with a client who designs and builds kiosks. Because they work with touch screen technology every day, they took it as a given that there are different types of touch technologies, each of which suits different uses. For example, emergency services workers need to have a screen that responds to a touch from a gloved finger. This company assumed that people looking for kiosks would know this (and maybe some of them did); however, when I worked with them, I helped them see that this information was worth sharing with their target audience. We wrote an article for their website about the different touch screen technologies, how they worked, and the uses for each one. This then inspired some other articles about kiosk-related print options and ergonomics, which positioned them as experts in every aspect of kiosk design and manufacture.

Given what we now know about timing—that is, you have to put yourself in front of your audience at the right moment for them to decide to take action—newsletters are a great way to stay in your audience's line of vision, prompting them to take that next step

Remember, your audience doesn't know what they don't know, and they may feel awkward at admitting they don't know it. It is a brave person who will admit their ignorance and ask a question about your solution. So, by sharing your information before your audience has to ask for it, you not only save them from embarrassment, but you also get to establish your leadership by introducing them to your great idea.

It's also worth noting that when you share information, it doesn't all have to be original material written by you. You can add great value to your audience by acting as a curator and sharing useful information that you believe your prospective customers will find interesting. The key here is to add your insights to the content you assemble, so that you are still establishing your own credibility and expertise in sharing the work of others.

Remember that articles are perfect for repurposing. You can use them in multiple ways—on your website, as a newsletter article, and on LinkedIn.

SELECTING TOPICS

Here's a quick summary of ideas for finding topics:

1) Observations

Share what you observe about your industry.

2) Solving a New Problem

Share your ideas on how to solve an emerging issue. This could be a follow-up article from a piece on industry observations.

3) Interpreting Someone Else's Useful Information

Don't feel that the information has to be your own original research. If you come across some useful third-party information and can contextualise it with your own commentary, that is just as useful to your audience. They'll remember that you brought it to their attention, and they may even associate you with the information more than they do the original author.

4) Giving a Taste of Your 'Secret Sauce'

Share useful information that educates your target audience about the skills that you offer the market.

5) Commonly Asked Questions

Think about the questions you are most often asked by customers and prospects and write an article that answers them.

6) Step-By-Step

Turn your business process into an article and take your readers through each step, explaining why it is important.

7) Why

Explain why you do what you do and tell the story behind your business. This can be a good way to build a more personalised connection.

ARTICLES ARE NOT ADS

Remember what we said in Chapter 7 about how no one wants to read advertisements. It's important to ensure that your article is not a thinly veiled (or even unveiled) ad. The role of an article is not to sell; it is to present information that shows you as an authority in your field.

5: NEWSLETTERS

The term 'newsletter' covers several formats. The key factor that differentiates this form of communication is that you are talking to a self-selected, subscribed audience. They have chosen to receive communication from you. The connection is already established, they know enough to want to hear more, and they have asked you to keep in touch.

Given what we now know about timing—that is, you have to put yourself in front of your audience at the right moment for them to decide to take action—newsletters are a great way to stay in your audience's line of vision, prompting them to take that next step.

A newsletter will contain some or all of the following elements.

INTRODUCTION

Given that you are speaking to a known audience on a regular basis, an introduction gives a personal and direct feel to your communication. It can be a short, simple, 'welcome to this edition' message; it can outline the articles they will read (if you have chosen to include multiple pieces); or it can relate to something topical.

ARTICLES/INSIGHTS

A newsletter is the perfect vehicle for sharing useful information, and it gives you a great opportunity to repurpose one or more of your blog articles.

One Article or Several

If you have plenty of content, but you have a less frequent newsletter schedule, you might want to include several articles in the same newsletter. I have a client who is a consulting firm, and their opinions are highly valued by their audience. Whilst they send out a newsletter only six times a year, they make sure to include three or four content-heavy articles in each one, giving their audience plenty of high-quality insights. This type of newsletter is a longer read, meant to be enjoyed over a cup of coffee, rather than skimmed at a glance.

If you communicate by newsletter more frequently, you'll want to include a single article per edition. It doesn't have to be long—in fact, one of the newsletters I really enjoy reading is just 200 to 300 words and shares one great idea or insight per edition.

So, how do you decide which format is best? The key is to know your audience and understand how they will read your newsletter. Do they want a two-minute read once a week or every fortnight? Or are they willing to settle in for a ten-minute review of your wisdom over their morning coffee once a month?

In Full or Summary Only

You can publish your whole article in your newsletter, or you can include a summary with a 'read more' link that takes the reader to your website for the full piece. There are pros and cons to each approach, so to determine which to use, return to your analysis of your target audience and their preferences.

Whether it's a formal introduction in a business meeting or a 'what do you do' moment at a barbecue, the elevator pitch is often your first chance to connect, and the words you say will impact the future of that connection. So, it is worth spending some time planning your response and having something ready to say.

For example, if you publish multiple articles in full, your newsletter might become unwieldy. In this format, I recommend including an executive summary at the top of your newsletter, which allows your reader to see the topics at a glance and choose what to read first.

On the other hand, the 'read more' approach invites people to visit your website, which could drive traffic to your site. One caveat here—think about the 'make it easy' tip from Chapter 8. If people have to click and wait (albeit a second) to go somewhere else to continue reading, you could lose them. (Personally, I get frustrated if I'm enjoying an article, and I have to stop to go somewhere else to finish it.)

My newsletter preference is to present a single article, in full, at a higher publication frequency. You can still include a call to action that sends readers to your website, but be aware that your click-through conversion rate will be dependent on the nature of your business and your subscribed audience.

OFFERS

Given that you have a subscribed audience, a newsletter is the perfect vehicle for promoting an offer without pushing it into 'hard sell' territory. For example, you can use your newsletter to share information about a new product launch or special pricing for an existing product. You can combine this into the same newsletter as your articles, or you can send a separate product offer newsletter (in this case, it falls under the category of 'eDM').

EVENTS AND COURSES

You can use specific newsletters to promote events, webinars, or education courses. Your subscribers get to be the first to know about your new offerings, which can increase their feelings of loyalty to you.

NEWS

If you decide to include a 'news' section, remember to present it in 'customer language'. If you've won an award, for example, there's nothing wrong with saying so, but make sure to present it in terms that relate to your audience (rather than making it all about how great you are). For example, you could turn this kind of announcement into a 'thank you' to all the customers who voted for you to win the award. Or if you're announcing that you've opened a new office location recently, you could write about how this will help you offer additional levels of service to your customers.

CALL TO ACTION

Remember the rule of no 'orphan communications'—make sure to include a call to action in your newsletter. This could be a link sending readers to your website, or it could be a simple 'get in touch' button that generates an email. If you are promoting a product or offer, it might be a link to a landing page for more information and sales. If your newsletter includes a single article in full, but you still want to generate website traffic, you could use a variation on the 'If you enjoyed this, you might also like...' approach, where you link to a couple of articles on your website and invite your audience to read them too.

6: PROPOSAL

When you are asked to provide a proposal, this is a clear indication that your 'Connect' and 'Convince' communication has done its job, but this is not the time to take your foot off the accelerator. Too many companies send out 'boilerplate' proposals—that is, a 'standard' document with no customisation, other than the client's contact information.

Let's make one thing clear—there is *no such thing* as a good boilerplate proposal.

A proposal is a summary that should be tailored to the business needs of an individual customer. It details how you can help them achieve their aspiration and/or solve their problem, and it describes the benefits you'll deliver. We know that benefits are 'in the eye of the beholder', so it stands to reason that a proposal must be individualised too. Personalising your communication is time consuming, but it is one of the best investments you can make.

There are two participants in a proposal—you and the prospective customer. You are the seller, and they are the buyer. A good proposal includes information for and about both, yet I have seen far too many proposals that only talk about the seller.

The structure I have outlined below ensures that both parties are represented in the proposal. The parts that are about you will not change greatly, in the sense that your offering will remain largely the same. The parts about the customer, however, may vary considerably and will need to be tailored.

1) TITLE

Your proposal should have a title, which is often tied to the benefits statement and/or the client's strategic goal.

2) THE CLIENT IN THEIR MARKETPLACE

Start your proposal by showing that you understand the client's environment—you know the market dynamics and changes in their industry, and you are familiar with the pressures and opportunities that shape their business. This also gives you a chance to recognise what the client is good at. Of course, you will still need to articulate the client's problem so you can present your solution, but no client appreciates having their shortcomings thrown at them 'cold'. So, think of this section as a 'warm up' before the 'problem' section.

3) WHAT IS THE ASPIRATION OR PROBLEM?

What is the client trying to achieve? What are the problems they face? These issues could be industry-wide or specific to the client's organisation.

You will need to validate this problem statement from outside your own organisation. The best ways of doing this are:

→ Using the client's own material.
  - The most direct source comes from your discussions with the client. Review your meeting notes, as well as any information they have told you about their business.
  - You can glean additional information from sources such as websites and annual reports.
  - Your client may not express their issue as a problem; they may instead present it as a strategic objective, a growth target, or a market position statement.
→ Using industry data, such as rankings or regulatory changes.
→ Using analysts' reports.

The aim of this section is to spell out the problem(s) that your client is facing. Be careful, however, that you don't overreach what your business can provide. Focus your solution on the problems for which your product or service provides an answer.

4) WHAT IS THE SOLUTION?

This is the first place that you mention your solution, in the form of your product or service. Outline the key elements (features) of your solution, but only include those that address the problem you have outlined above. Don't limit your description to the physical features of your solution. In fact, your real differentiation may lie in your pricing model, delivery service, or after-sales support.

After writing this section, go back round the problem/solution loop. There may be a feature of your product or service for which you haven't yet articulated the client's challenge. As you map out each client issue and your corresponding solution, add it to the problem statement. You should end up with a one-to-one match between problem statement and solution feature.

5) WHY CHOOSE US?

This is where you get to brag (and not before). The aim of this section is to show that you are the best—in fact, the only—choice to provide this solution. It is appropriate to detail your relevant experience, your successful projects, and the length of time your business has been providing this solution. You might include industry awards, growth success, and testimonials from your other delighted clients.

6) BENEFITS

In this section you are aiming to describe how your client's business will be different if they choose your solution. What will life look like once they have picked you and implemented your suggested approach? Make sure to refer back to the client's problem and contrast it with the 'new world' that you will provide. Validation here is in the form of projected savings, growth, customer satisfaction, ROI—whatever the appropriate measures are for your client's aspiration. Numbers speak louder than words, and they are important as they lead into the pricing section.

7) PRICING

For a proposed solution to be attractive, the benefits should outweigh the price, hence explaining the benefits immediately before the pricing. If the client perceives the pricing as too high, it could be because you have not sufficiently articulated the benefits.

Pricing should be laid out in an orderly structure, such as within a formatted table. Ensure you clarify whether pricing includes or excludes tax. You will also need to distinguish between one-off and ongoing costs. If the proposed solution consists of different elements, such as a product (one-off price) and a service (regular payments), make this evident and show these items separately.

As with the rest of your solution, think about the pricing from the client's point of view:

→ Consider whether you can structure the pricing to align with the delivery of the solution. It may be harder for the client to make a large upfront investment in a solution where the benefits come months or years later, so consider staged payments to coordinate cost and benefit.

→ Consider whether you can offer incentives, such as volume discounts or a 'loyalty' approach to your pricing. One caveat about incentives—beware of the 'new user' discount that companies often use. It risks attracting one-off purchasers, rather than a long-term, loyal customer base, and it may alienate existing customers.

8) CALL TO ACTION

One of the hardest parts of submitting a proposal is getting the client to take the next step. So, it is important to determine beforehand what you want that next step to be. Then, ask your client to take it. The goal here is to be unambiguous about what you want the client to do. This may sound obvious, but many business proposals have a weak close that leaves clients scratching their heads about the next steps to take.

Are you asking the client to accept and sign the proposal? In this case, include an acceptance form with the proposal so they can sign it there and then.

Are you asking the client to book a meeting where you will present your proposal to them? Or to schedule a date to start a trial? Or to meet about building a project plan? In this case, give them a link to an online calendar/booking system and direct them to choose a time to meet with you.

The key is to make it 100% clear what you are asking for and make it as easy as possible for the client to do it.

Finally, finish on a strong sales message—tie it back to the title of your proposal, which is based on the client's benefits. Remember, everything hinges on the benefits.

PROPOSAL STRUCTURE

If this structure looks familiar—it is. (And you've clearly been paying attention!) With the exception of the pricing section, it is essentially the same format as your strategy, as outlined in Chapter 4. I also used a modified version of this structure in Chapter 1. That is the beauty of this approach—when you create a message strategy, you can use it time and time again.

A note about tenders vs. proposals. The structure outlined above is used when you're asked to provide a proposal—that is, in your own format. If you respond to a formal tender, you will need to follow the buyer's structure by answering the questions they ask. However, you will almost always have the opportunity to begin with an executive summary, and for that, you can use the above structure. For example, starting with the client's context and aspirations is much more engaging than the tired old 'thank you for the opportunity to respond'.

7: CASE STUDIES

Remember learning to write stories at school? Your teachers taught you that a story has a beginning, middle, and end. Well, a case study follows that same basic format.

CASE STUDY STRUCTURE

A case study is simply a way of putting what you offer into a story—a story where one of your existing clients is the hero. A case study therefore follows a simple structure.

Beginning

This is where you set the scene, providing some background about the story's 'hero' and their challenge. Include details to help your reader relate to the hero, such as industry, location, and company size. Then describe the hero's aspiration and the problem that was stopping them from reaching it.

Middle

This is where you tell the story of what you did for the client. Explain the product or service you delivered to address their issue.

End

This is the outcome. You get to describe the difference that your solution made for the client. Ideally, this section will include measurable results (e.g. 'Our solution reduced the cost of XYZ by 10%') to prove the value of what you did.

Summary

This section sums up the problem and benefits.

THE VOICE

A case study is presented in the voice of the customer. If you write about what you did without input from the customer, it is not a case study.

Interview the customer to capture their words or engage a third party to conduct the interview. Then you can edit this customer statement into a quotable narrative that tells the story of working with you.

When you interview the customer, I recommend that you ask them just four questions.

→   The first three questions mirror the story structure:

1) 'Tell me about what you were aiming to achieve and what was stopping you', OR 'Tell me about the issues you were facing.'

2) 'Tell me about what XYZ company did for you?' OR 'What was the solution that XYZ company delivered?'

3) 'What was the result?' OR 'How did that change your business?'

→ The fourth question that I recommend is:

4) 'Tell me the three best things about XYZ company'. This sometimes elicits new information, or it confirms what the client believes were the most important aspects of the story. The answer to this question can provide a good summary.

REPURPOSING

Case studies are a wonderful source for repurposing. They can become:

→ An article in your newsletter.
→ A blog on your website.
→ The 'outcomes' section of a presentation.
→ Short testimonial quotes on your website or in a brochure (extract one or two sentences of the customer's own words).
→ A LinkedIn article.
→ A LinkedIn short post—using a testimonial quote, for example.
→ The 'customer story' part of your elevator pitch, summarised into a few sentences.

8: PRESENTATIONS

Being invited to present to an audience is a fantastic opportunity. As we saw in Chapter 5, it can be a chance to connect, convince, and even convert, all in one format. Yet some businesses don't make the most of this opportunity—maybe you are even one of them.

Some people think of a presentation as a 'show' rather than a form of communication. They get anxious about how they will 'perform' and forget that a presentation is an opportunity for two-way communication with an audience.

Others have the 'I'll just wing it' approach, believing that there is a 'presentation magic' that suddenly turns their underprepared ideas into a logical, intelligible, articulate flow. I have never met anyone who presents better 'off the cuff'. The people who make speaking look effortless are the ones who've put in the most effort.

The third group of people spend some time preparing and have good ideas to share, but they don't have a clear structure. Using our earlier analogy, they have the decorations, but no Christmas tree. This results in a string of slides with no clear story or flow.

A presentation is like an iceberg—90% of the work that goes into it is unseen. In other words, nine-tenths of a successful presentation is based on what you do before you stand up and open your mouth—and that means doing three things: planning, preparation, and practice.

Planning is simply working out the outcomes you want to achieve—what do you want your audience to feel, know, and do based on your presentation? Unless you have planned what a successful outcome looks like, how will you know if you have achieved it? So, think about the emotion you want to engender (what you want the audience to feel), the information you want to impart (what you want them to know), and the action you're looking for (what you want them to do).

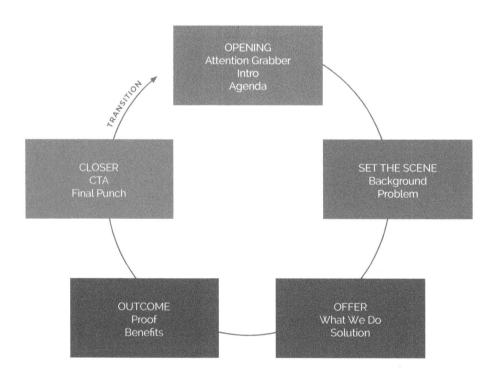

Preparation is where structure comes in. The presentation structure that I recommend has five elements. It helps you to:

→ Ensure that your presentation has a logical flow and tells a story.

→ Know where you are and where you're going next, so your audience can easily follow you.

→ Create a basic (ten minute) presentation, which you can then extend to any length without changing the structure—you simply expand or contract the content in each of the blocks.

1: OPENING

A great starting point is an 'attention grabber'. Whilst there's nothing wrong with starting by introducing yourself and your agenda, the attention grabber ensures that your audience is with you right from the start, interested and eager to hear more. It can be a story that pertains to your topic, a relatable statement, a quote, a joke, or a question. Then you introduce yourself (you can repurpose from your elevator pitch) and present your agenda.

2: SET THE SCENE

This is where you paint a picture of the aspiration, problem, or solution. If your audience doesn't believe or understand the problem, they won't have any interest in hearing about the solution.

3: THE OFFER

This is where you get to talk about what you do. It's the part that speakers tend to be most comfortable with, and many presentations actually start (and end) here. However, as I hope you can see, by setting the scene first, you make your offer a lot more engaging. In the section on articles above, I shared with you several approaches, such as the list and the pendulum—these also work well as mechanisms for explaining your offer.

4: THE OUTCOMES

As we've seen throughout this book, customers buy benefits, and outcomes are what inspire action. Even if the benefits are obvious to you, it's important to state them explicitly to your audience. You can bring your benefits to life by telling customer stories—the greater the similarity between your audience and the customer in the story, the more they will relate.

5: THE CLOSER

This is where you get to ask for something. In your planning, you've decided what you want your audience to do, so now you ask for it. This is not necessarily asking for the sale—that will depend on where you are with this audience on the customer journey—but it will be something that keeps them engaged with you. It could be an invitation to an event, asking them to subscribe to a newsletter, or offering a demonstration. The important thing is to ask them to take some sort of action. When you ask your audience to take a small action now, they will be more likely to engage with you in greater ways later. Finally, if you can refer back to your 'attention grabber', it will round off your presentation with a professional flourish.

TRANSITIONS

Transitions take your presentation from a series of unrelated ideas to a logical story. For example, a transition from Offer to Outcomes might go something like this: 'We've looked at [the solution], but you might be wondering, "Does it work?" Yes, it does, so let me show you how.'

A final word on presentations—it's a big topic, and I have only touched on the bare essentials here. If you'd like more detail, do get in touch for a copy of my eBook, *Present with Panache*.

9: LINKEDIN

You've no doubt got a LinkedIn profile and have used it to find, connect with, and convince your ideal audience.

The effectiveness of your LinkedIn as a form of business communication depends on what's in your profile. There's a lot of competition for your audience's attention, so if you want your profile to work for you as a communication tool, it's worth spending some time ensuring it has the content to do its job.

Remember that there are two different audiences for a LinkedIn profile. You might be looking for a new job and therefore communicating with recruiters and potential employers (LinkedIn started as a recruitment platform, and many people still use it in that way). For our purposes, however, let's assume that you are targeting the other audience—potential clients. This means that your profile must communicate your value, make a connection, and convince your prospects.

HEADLINE

Think of your headline as a condensed elevator pitch. Ideally, it should give readers a quick flavour of who you help and how. Many people simply put their job title, but they're missing an important message opportunity.

There are two alternative styles used in headlines:

→ A short sentence, such as, 'Helping [target audience] to [outcome/benefit]'.

→ A string of descriptors, such as, 'Innovator | Entrepreneur | Inventor | Fishing fanatic'. (Some people like to throw in a personal or amusing descriptor—this is where you could use your Superhero Name from the elevator pitch).

As with the elevator pitch, the more precise you can be about identifying who you are talking to, the more your message will resonate with its intended audience.

PHOTO

Profiles with a photo are, according to LinkedIn's own data, fourteen times more likely to be reviewed than those without. If a prospective client is looking for you and they find a profile with no photo, it can look as if you have something to hide.

The right photo is important too. Make sure that it is a well-lit headshot with an expression that matches the message from you and your business. (E.g. 'professional but approachable', or 'individualistic and innovative'.) Photos are one of those things that everyone thinks they can do, but I personally feel that using a professional photographer is worth every cent that you pay. An unprofessional looking photo doesn't help you and can even make your prospects less likely to get in touch. If you really want to use your own photo, my guidance is to avoid the '3 Ps':

→ **No Parties:** Your audience needs to see you in a 'work' environment, not a social setting.

→ **No Partners:** Avoid those photos that have an 'orphan hand' on your shoulder where you have cut out the person next to you.

→ **No Peering:** Your photo should be a head and shoulders shot. If you have a full body shot, your face will appear so small that it is barely recognisable. (I once spent ages trying to work out if I had the right contact on LinkedIn, as his photo was taken from a distance, and he was wearing a bicycle helmet.)

ABOUT

Along with the headline, the 'About' section may be the only part of your profile that prospects will read. This summary sets the scene for how they will think and feel about continuing the customer journey with you.

The wording in your 'About' section can be repurposed from your positioning statement (which in turn is a variation on your elevator pitch). It can have up to 2000 characters.

A good outline template is:

1. One sentence summary of your value.
2. Problem statement or relatable question, referring to your target audience as specifically as you can.
3. How you solve the problem.
4. Benefits of working with you.
5. Your credentials.
6. Call to action.

Don't forget the tips we covered in Chapters 6 and 7. For example, weave your 'Why' into your 'About' section, and use facts and statistics in your profile where you can.

One of the most common traps people fall into when writing their 'About' section is forgetting which of the two LinkedIn audiences they are addressing. When you are talking to your prospective clients, your message needs to be centred around the ways that you add value for them.

For example, many people talk about how motivated they are, how they consistently exceed their sales targets, and what a great leader they are. Whilst that might interest an employer (and even then, it would be better couched in terms of how you will add value to the company), it is not what your prospective clients need to hear.

Another common mistake people make is metaphorically 'shouting'. On LinkedIn, a profile that 'shouts' is one that throws around superlatives with no evidence, or uses overworked, bland phrases. 'Self-motivated', 'good team player', and 'results-driven sales manager' come to mind as repeat offenders.

EXPERIENCE

This is a list of your current and previous job roles. Your current position is the most important, and whilst the title here can be your job role, the description should include who and how you help, not just a list of tasks. As you go back further through your working history, you need less detail about each role.

One tip here—when you put in the name of your company, link it to the LinkedIn profile for that organisation. That way, their logo will show in your profile, which looks more professional than the default grey-coloured boxes.

RECOMMENDATIONS

As we learnt in Chapter 7, the words of others are worth more than your own. LinkedIn recognises this fact and enables you to publish people's recommendations of you and your solution. You may receive them unsolicited, or you can ask for them—in fact, if you are doing a case study with a happy client, you can ask them to repeat some of their comments in a recommendation. Once again, we see the power of repurposing!

The other sections are useful, as well, so fill them out as you have time, but focus on the ones described above.

ARTICLES AND POSTS

LinkedIn is not just a place to share your profile; it is also a platform for publishing your content. You can repurpose your blogs as LinkedIn articles. You can also write short posts to generate interest in an article, to promote an event, or simply to maintain a conversation with your contacts.

You may want to share other people's content too. In this case, be sure to add your own short commentary to increase its value and promote your own thought leadership.

For tips on how to create the other sections of your profile, get in touch for a copy of my eBook, *Building a Great LinkedIn Profile*.

Too many companies send out 'boilerplate' proposals — that is, a 'standard' document with no customisation, other than the client's contact information.

Let's make one thing clear — there is no such thing as a good boilerplate proposal.

10: EBOOKS

An eBook is one of the best ways to convince your audience that you are an expert in your field. It gives you more scope than an article, and it is often based on research, harnessing the convincing power of facts and statistics. An eBook can also be effective during the 'Connect' stage, helping your audience to find you as they search for answers to their pressing questions.

Profiles with a photo are, according to LinkedIn's own data, fourteen times more likely to be reviewed than those without. If a prospective client is looking for you and they find a profile with no photo, it can look as if you have something to hide.

Like an article, an eBook should not be an advert. It is an opportunity to discuss a topic of interest and share insights. It will have your company name on it, and readers will know it comes from you (otherwise, how will they know you're the expert?), but it is not about overtly pushing products or services.

There are many structural approaches you can take when you create an eBook. Two of the most popular and effective are the 'Research' eBook and the 'How-To' eBook.

RESEARCH EBOOK

1: Introduction and Summary

Think back to the inverted pyramid we discussed in Chapter 7, as well as the 'before and after' versions of the letter that illustrated the importance of presenting the key information up front. This first section of your eBook engages the audience by telling them what they can expect during their read. Here, you lay out the premise, such as the aspiration or problem you address, and you introduce your solutions to the issue.

2: Research

This is where you set the scene, using research to back up your statements. This could be your own research, but most often it draws on information from external, reputable sources. Look for reports that back up your position. In this section, you will paint a picture of the situation or trends, so using external research adds gravitas and credibility to your key points. (You should always cite your sources using a standardised style guide, such as the Snooks & Co. Style Manual in Australia or The Oxford Guide to Style in the UK.)

3: Interpretation

This is the 'So What' part of your eBook. It's where you translate the research-backed description of a situation into an opportunity for your audience. The more specific you make it to their industry, the more impact your eBook will have.

4: Answer

The 'Answer' section explains how your audience can make the most of the opportunity or address the issue. Remember, you are not explicitly promoting your solution; you are sharing your expertise.

5: Conclusion

Summarise the research, the interpretation, and the answer, and provide a way for the reader to get in touch for further discussion.

THE HOW-TO EBOOK

Another popular format is a guidebook that shows your audience a step-by-step process for how to complete a specific task. This kind of eBook illustrates how to accomplish something they would have otherwise found difficult. It may also demonstrate how the reader will save time and money by engaging your services instead of doing the task themselves. In this way, a How-To eBook can also be part of your 'Convert' strategy.

1: Introduction

Outline what the task is, why it is important, and why people find it difficult. Explain the benefits they'll get from reading this eBook, in that the knowledge contained within will make them better equipped to carry out the task at hand.

2: Step-By-Step

Take them through the key steps in the process. If these steps are reasonably short (a few sentences each), you can do this as a numbered list. If the steps take longer to describe, you might need to dedicate a section or a chapter to each one. As you introduce each step, explain why it's important and how to approach it.

3: Conclusion

Summarise the importance of the process and restate the benefits of your step-by-step instructions.

You can use sections or a summary of your eBook as a newsletter article or a LinkedIn post.

A WORD ABOUT DESIGN

Throughout this chapter, I've focussed on the importance of the words you use in these ten business formats. Effective communication, however, relies as much on compelling visual design as it does on well-written sentences. This is particularly true for your website, presentation slides, newsletter, and eBooks.

Hiring a professional graphic designer is not a 'nice to have'; rather, your designer is an essential part of your team. Good graphic design and layout leads the eye through the document and significantly increases readability. It enhances your words and makes them more likely to be read and remembered. Since design contributes to your communication's ability to connect, convince, and convert, I strongly recommend engaging a professional graphic designer with years of expertise in the field.

SINCE DESIGN CONTRIBUTES TO YOUR COMMUNICATION'S ABILITY TO CONNECT, CONVINCE, AND CONVERT, I STRONGLY RECOMMEND ENGAGING A PROFESSIONAL GRAPHIC DESIGNER WITH YEARS OF EXPERTISE IN THE FIELD.

NEXT STEPS

We've now looked at some of the practical ways you can take the tips and strategies in this book and turn them into effective communication formats for your business. I am sure that if you've read this far, you know what's coming in the next chapter—we are going to demonstrate the benefits of this process. So, read on to see how other tech companies have successfully applied the Connect, Convince, Convert approach. I'll show you how transforming their business communication has helped these companies to create happy, loyal customers

CAROL BENTON

10

Success Stories

LET'S RECAP

I've spoken throughout this book of the importance of articulating the benefits of a solution, and this is where I practice what I preach. In this chapter, I will articulate the benefits of the Connect, Convince, Convert approach. We'll take a look at five of the greatest benefits, with real-life examples of organisations who have reaped these rewards.

As we've seen, Connect, Convince, Convert is not about making a quick sale or pushing a prospect into something they're not ready for and may ultimately regret. It's a process that builds a connection, forges a relationship, generates trust, and leads naturally to doing business. It requires you to take active steps to guide the prospect, but it means that the decision to engage in business with you is the client's own. If you follow the process successfully, your prospects will want to purchase your products and services, rather than feeling cajoled or dragged into a decision.

This process also helps you to filter out those who are not the ideal client early on, saving you from spending time and effort on the 'wrong' audience. Whilst Connect, Convince, Convert may take a little longer than other systems, it ultimately leads to greater outcomes, helping you transform your clients into loyal advocates of your solution.

1: PLANNING AHEAD TO PREVENT COSTLY MISTAKES

Spending time up front on creating a strategy saves a great deal of time, cost, and wasted opportunity. It ensures that your communication is consistent, no matter what the medium or format. Consistency, as we have seen, is an important part of credibility.

Having a strategy behind your message reduces the chances of 'mis-communications'—that is, communications which don't tie in with your overall message. At best, these communications might leave your audience feeling a bit confused. At worst, your audience will put you in the 'too hard' basket and move on, losing you potential business.

If you were going on a trip, you'd spend time planning your route, rather than just working it out as you go along. Without a plan, you risk taking the wrong route or catching the slower train, which will cost you more time than you would have spent in preparation.

To use another analogy, ask any tradesman and they'll tell you their mantra is 'measure twice, cut once'. That is, it's worth taking the time to be sure that everything is correct before you take an action that is irreversible. In the case of communication, the irreversible action doesn't simply result in a wasted piece of timber or a pipe that is too short. Instead, when you fail to connect, it impacts your audience's judgement of you, placing a roadblock in their path towards becoming a loyal advocate of your business.

CLIENT OUTCOME

Not long after completing a message strategy, a client said to me, 'I love that I don't have to reinvent the wheel every time I communicate'. The trigger for his comment was that the company was exhibiting at a trade show, and the organisers had asked for a 50–100-word overview of the company to go in the event catalogue. (Yes, this was a small piece of content, but as we have discussed, the shorter forms of communication are often the hardest to write because every word must carry its weight.)

He asked if I could help him write this description, but I reminded him that he already had it. As part of his message strategy, we had developed a positioning statement (a written version of the elevator pitch). It was a short summary of the company's value—who they helped, what they offered, and the outcomes their solution delivered. This was a lightbulb moment for him—he didn't need to 'reinvent the wheel'; all he had to do was repurpose his existing content.

If you were going on a trip, you'd spend time planning your route, rather than just working it out as you go along. Without a plan, you risk taking the wrong route or catching the slower train, which will cost you more time than you would have spent in preparation.

My engagement with this client had started when he heard me speak at a conference about the importance of effective communication for technology companies. I spoke about the need for a message strategy, and I shared some tips on getting from 'what' to 'so what'. They were going through a transformative time in their business, and the need for a strong message strategy really struck home. They realised that the end result of all the internal work they were doing had to be communicated to their target audience. If they were changing the way they served the market, they knew they needed to change their messaging too.

I facilitated a message strategy workshop, where we walked through the five key questions from Chapter 4. This process helped them articulate what they did, for whom, and why. I documented the outcomes into a written message strategy, which became the foundation for all their communications, including that short description in the event catalogue.

We validated their thinking with a customer survey. It comprised a series of interviews that I carried out with their clients to get the most important perspective—that of the people who were already using their product and service. Their input was used to further refine the strategy.

With the message strategy in place, we were able to get on with the job of refreshing their communications—elevator pitch, website, blogs, brochures, proposals, and presentations—without, as the client put it, 'reinventing the wheel every time'. Having a clear message was useful internally too; it ensured that all staff were 'singing from the same hymn sheet'. This meant that every form of communication was focussed, which helped the company's message remain consistent, giving it credibility in all formats. Their customers now understand what they offer and the value it delivers.

Without this clear strategy, my client realised that his company would have needed to 'start from scratch' each and every time they wanted to communicate in a new format.

In fact, a clue that you need to spend more time on your strategy is if you are struggling to create each piece of communication, and you find yourself reinventing the wheel every time. It is an indication that you need to go through another iteration of your strategy planning to fine tune the detail.

The time spent on a message strategy is an investment that will pay you back multiple times over. It will ensure that when you do communicate, you do so in a way that enhances your brand and your reputation. Your strategy will add to a consistent and clear portrayal of your business and your value. By creating your message once and then propagating it many times across all your communication formats, you will save yourself time and money.

2: BUILDING STRONG AND LOYAL RELATIONSHIPS

We're not New York souvenir sellers, caught in the cycle of sell, move on, sell, move on. We're after long-term relationships with customers who want to stick with us and tell others about our value. The

Connect, Convince, Convert process will help you to create those strong and loyal relationships. Doing business with clients who return time and time again and who refer you to others is more cost effective than having to find new clients each time because your existing ones move on.

Following the steps outlined in the previous chapters will ensure that you connect with emotion—that is, with the part of your audience's brain that makes a decision. You will connect with the person, not just the company. This starts with digging into the 'why' of your business. Once you're able to share that consistent, authentic message with your prospects, you will reap the rewards in the form of an enthusiastic and devoted customer base.

CLIENT OUTCOME

I work with a client whose key differentiator is their people. They sell a wide range of products, most of which are manufactured by other organisations, so the value they add is in having staff who can help customers through the maze of technology options and put together the best solution. Their staff are known for their expertise, dedication, professionalism, and sense of fun.

They approached me to learn how they could make this their point of difference. Customers and prospects who met them or spoke to them on the phone were always impressed, but the company wanted to be able to convey their personalised service and in-depth knowledge via their website as well. They wanted to sow the seeds of differentiation right from the moment someone searched for them online. Their goal was to highlight their people as a way to set themselves apart from their competitors, who simply showcased products.

I helped them by carrying out short interviews with all their key, customer-facing staff and writing a concise, tailored biography of each of them. Now when new members join the team, their profiles are added to the site. These 'pen portraits' share each person's professional background and skills, what they love in their current role, and how they help their clients. They have a photo to make them more immediate, speaking directly to the audience. The profiles have a slightly quirky, personal flavour, which reflects the organisation. Above all, it creates emotion and a sense of connection. The profiles have been well received and have become a bit of a talking point. This company now has some of the most loyal customers I have seen in any organisation.

Selling technology can sometimes feel like an impersonal experience, but by using the Connect, Convince, Convert approach, you can change this. The key is in finding and sharing the passion behind your business. People want to buy from a brand where they feel a connection, and they seek out companies they feel tied to and can get behind. If you can use this approach to create that connection, you'll benefit from having strong relationships with clients who don't buy on price; instead, they buy on relationship and conviction. They will return time and time again, and tell others about you, increasing your revenue and your profitability.

3: ELIMINATING THE COMPETITION

In an ideal world, we'd be in a category of one, with no competition. Our clients would see us as the only choice, and they would make their decision based on value rather than cost. Conversion would be almost effortless, and the decision to work with us would be one they would feel compelled to make as 'the only option'.

Using the Connect, Convince, Convert process helps you to elevate your business and get closer to being in that enviable 'category of one'. Once you start to share useful information, you position yourself as an expert in your field. 'Expert' is not an easy position for a competitor to take away from you. Your prospects will see you as the go-to person. You become someone that your customers trust, want to work with, and will seek out for advice. They value what you can offer and are less likely to walk away and transact with someone else.

With the message strategy in place, we were able to get on with the job of refreshing their communications—elevator pitch, website, blogs, brochures, proposals, and presentations—without, as the client put it, 'reinventing the wheel every time'.

By following the principles of sharing your expertise, you raise yourself above a generic sales conversation that asks prospects, 'Here's my product, here's a great price, do you want to buy it?' Instead, you engage your clients in a tailored discussion, telling them, 'I understand you want to achieve a specific outcome, so here are some thoughts on how you can do it'. This means not having to do a hard sell on smaller packages, and it leads to a relationship that provides 'big picture' solutions.

Using the words of others is another element of Connect, Convince, Convert that helps to elevate your presence. Nothing says 'this company is good at what it does' better than the words of someone who has put you to the test and been delighted with the outcome. If a prospect reads about how you've helped someone just like them, that automatically elevates you and puts you into an exclusive category. This amplifies the connection between you and the prospect, which reduces price sensitivity.

CLIENT OUTCOME

A technology company approached me looking for help in positioning themselves as experts. They had several target markets, so they needed to speak to each one in its own language, addressing the problems they faced and the benefits they could expect. There was no 'one size fits all' message. In order to succeed, this company had to be seen as experts in healthcare by the healthcare sector, education by the education sector, and hospitality by the hospitality sector.

I helped them to develop content that discussed the key issues faced by each of their target verticals, explaining how each issue could be addressed with the company's technology. These articles didn't overtly 'sell' their product; rather, they focussed on the technology and what it delivered. There was always a call to action so readers knew where to go next, but the overall theme of the content was the sharing of information that the target audience would find valuable. We interspersed these articles with case studies to enhance the expert positioning with practical evidence of their approach.

This organisation places their articles in industry publications for each of their key verticals. They've done the background work and understand where their target audiences go for information, what they read, and the sources they find credible. They understand who else influences their audiences, and some of their content is specifically aimed at those recommenders and influencers.

This content strategy is helping my client elevate their position in the market. It works because the articles showcase the *benefits* of their approach and their technology. They are not 'selling' in their articles or publishing ads; instead, they are sharing genuinely useful information.

CLIENT OUTCOME

Another tech company I work with has used communication to elevate themselves from hardware seller to solution provider. They have recently expanded their portfolio with the addition of a software solution. This has enabled them to differentiate themselves and rise above the 'feature and price' selling that is widespread in their niche of the hardware market. They have several target audiences, so they use a different 'flavour' of their solution for each.

I've been able to help them develop targeted web pages, brochures, and eBooks that talk specifically to each of these groups, articulating the business issues they face and the ways that my client's solution can address these problems. These communications elevate my client out of the pack and into a significantly smaller pool. They open up discussions that enable the company to position themselves as solution experts, not simply sellers of hardware. This brings them closer to the goal of becoming 'the only option.'

4: INCREASING YOUR CONVERSION RATE

'We need more leads' is a mantra that you'll hear from many companies. However, sifting through leads is time-consuming and expensive. The less qualified they are, the more work they require. Companies that focus purely on lead quantity end up having to dedicate far more resources to the conversion process.

The Connect, Convince, Convert approach embodies the principle that ten well-qualified leads are worth more than 100 random enquiries. This shifts the focus from quantity to quality. In fact, by using this process, your leads will pretty much qualify themselves, saving you time, effort, and money.

Defining who your audience is, what their issues are, and how you help them allows you to speak directly to the people who need you. You'll be 'using their name' and reflecting their requirements back to them. This necessarily means that there will be people who visit your website, read your article, or look at your brochure and say, 'not for me.' Although it might seem counter-intuitive (especially if your focus has been on quantity of leads), this is exactly what you want. If the people who are not your target audience recognise this themselves, it means they will not waste your time by getting in touch, only to be qualified out by you. You are effectively 'outsourcing' much of your qualification process to your audience.

The people who do 'see themselves' in your communications will be the right fit. There will be no need to go through the frustrating process of trying to shape the potential customer to you, or you to them. No square pegs in round holes; you will already be aligned.

Ill-qualified leads often try to negotiate you into providing the solution they want, pulling you in all directions. However, if you have done the work at the strategy stage to pinpoint your ideal client, shaping your communication around them, you will have a match made in heaven.

Well-qualified prospects don't have as many feature and price concerns, and the process of convincing and converting them becomes a great deal less time consuming, frustrating, and costly. If you could convert 50% of ten well qualified leads, rather than 2% of your random enquiries, you'd not only have more clients, but you'd have won them with much less 'wasted' effort on your part.

CLIENT OUTCOME

A software company that I work with has several target audiences in different industry sub-segments, and they wanted to tailor their communication specifically to each audience.

I have been able to help them by creating content in the form of articles, newsletters, and eBooks. The content is effective because it is regular, consistent, and targeted.

Regularity helps to build up awareness and presence; it ensures that even if a recipient isn't ready the first time they receive the message, they will hear it again once the timing is right. Consistency, as we know, builds credibility and helps to forge a relationship. Speaking directly to the reader leaves no doubt in their mind as to whether they are the target audience. If someone who is in your target audience reads your article, they will understand straight away that it's for them. Someone outside that audience might well enjoy reading it and learn something from it, but they would not be driven to get in touch, as it would be clear that the message is not addressed to them. The regular, consistent, and targeted content I've helped this client produce has brought in leads that are already self-qualified.

The aim of business communication is ultimately to get someone to say 'yes'. If you start with an audience that you wish to serve, and that wants and can afford your offering, you will make it easier for all parties to do business in a way that benefits everyone.

PEOPLE WANT TO BUY FROM A BRAND WHERE THEY FEEL A CONNECTION, AND THEY SEEK OUT COMPANIES THEY FEEL TIED TO AND CAN GET BEHIND. IF YOU CAN USE THIS APPROACH TO CREATE THAT CONNECTION, YOU'LL BENEFIT FROM HAVING STRONG RELATIONSHIPS WITH CLIENTS WHO DON'T BUY ON PRICE; INSTEAD, THEY BUY ON RELATIONSHIP AND CONVICTION.

5: CREATING HAPPIER CUSTOMERS

We all feel happier doing something that is our own decision, rather than something we feel we have been pushed into. One of the benefits of the Connect, Convince, Convert process is the way that customers feel when they engage with you. They have been drawn towards you by a shared connection, and they are convinced that you understand them and can help them. When they ultimately decide to do business with you, it is a natural outcome of this process; you haven't compelled them with a hard sell that gets them to buy but leaves them feeling uncomfortable with their action.

When you use this process, your target audience is more likely to find you, rather than you having to go out and track them down. This is what marketing and social media expert Andrew Ford calls 'e-ttraction'.[1] Since you are clear about who you're talking to, they know your message is aimed at them, and they're more likely to want to enter into a conversation. Your goal is for your audience to self-qualify themselves in or out, so you don't need to cajole them into something that's not right for them (or you). Instead, you can show them how other organisations just like them have benefitted from working with you, making them keen to find out more. Rather than pushing your offer at them, you gently pull them towards you. Since you have taken the time to 'marinate' in conversion, they feel pleased with their decision to engage, instead of pressured.

The success of this process is due to the prospective client having a greater degree of control in the whole journey. Of course, you are initiating the actions and creating the communication, but because your message is centred on your audience and their goals, aspirations, and objectives, they are naturally attracted to it.

CLIENT OUTCOME

A technology services client of mine has been able to reach this enviable position. I helped them with a message strategy, which we then implemented with a range of communication formats, enticing customers to learn more. We developed a new website that focussed on benefits to create instant engagement and interest. We shared customer stories to build connection and credibility, and we created articles that showcased my client's expertise in their field.

---

[1] Ford, Andrew. Creating a Powerful Brand. Social Star. 2014.

This organisation doesn't have to go out and chase business; instead, customers come to them, based on the content they have published, or on the recommendation of other delighted clients. They do have to put in some effort, of course—they follow up to maintain the connection with their prospects, and they marinate in the convince process. However, they are not driven by FOMO (the fear of missing out) or the scarcity principle—they are not tempted to do business with unsuitable clients due to the absence of any other options. This has greatly reduced the time they spend on 'chasing up' reluctant contacts, and it has transformed many of their well-qualified prospects into satisfied customers. And as they have learnt, satisfied customers spend more, return more frequently, and refer to other prospects.

IN SUMMARY

You are a technology expert, and you have invested a great deal in creating your solutions. But even the best technology needs a bit of help if it's to be the foundation of a thriving business. The difference between great tech and a great business is communication. The Connect, Convince, Convert process allows you to bridge that gap.

By planning your strategy, you will know the precise identity of your target customer, and you won't have to reinvent the wheel each time you communicate with them. You'll create solid relationships with clients who not only return to you time and again, but who also become your best generators of well-qualified leads. You'll screen your prospects, making it easier to talk to people and companies who understand what you offer and know that you can help them.

You'll elevate yourself and your business to 'expert' status, and you'll avoid having to jump on the 'me too', or the 'I can do it for less' bandwagon. You'll have customers coming to you and feeling good about doing so because they know they're going to receive a solution that delivers real value to their business.

By following the processes outlined in this book, you and your company can realise these benefits, just like the clients whose stories I've shared in this chapter. You'll create sparks of connection that grow into flames of conviction and build into a furnace that shapes your prospects into loyal customers.

Above all, as the sub-title of this book says, Connect, Convince, Convert will help you, as a great technology company, harness the power of words to win more business.

AFTERWORD

A few years ago, I went on a trek in the Himalayas, up to Everest Base Camp and back. We spent sixteen days hiking, camping, and marvelling at the majesty of our surroundings. We passed the time keeping warm, protecting ourselves against altitude sickness, making friendships, and learning about the region from our amazing team of Sherpas. We trekkers came from suburban lives in the UK, US, Australia, Canada, and New Zealand, so every part of the journey was outside our previous experience. It was all new, exciting, and overwhelming—a lot to process in two weeks.

When we got back to Kathmandu, the trekkers and Sherpas in our party gathered for a 'final night dinner'. The head Sherpa led us in a conversation about the journey we'd taken together—what we'd seen, heard, tasted, experienced, and learnt. This turned out to be a vital part of the trip—it was a chance to pause, review, and process all the new experiences and information. It helped me to seal the experiences within my memory, to put the events into context, and to step back and see the journey as a whole.

When you are in the moment, focussing (literally) on putting one foot in front of the other, it is hard to see the bigger picture of where you're going and where you've been. As my group hiked up to Everest Base Camp, the sheer scale of our surroundings dwarfed everything else. It was nothing short of magnificent, but it was also a weird mix of sensory overload combined with a rapid visual 'acclimatisation' that resulted in us growing accustomed to waking up surrounded by the highest peaks on the planet.

The final night dinner was an opportunity to review the journey with a different perspective. It translated my step-by-step experience into a bird's-eye map of the whole route that I could contextualise for myself and communicate to others. It gave me a clear understanding of what I had just gone through, and it provided me with the words to explain it better to my family and friends when I got home. It even inspired me to encourage others to set out on their own adventures. It was the perfect close to a great journey.

Sometimes you need a 'final night dinner' after a book—a chance to congratulate yourself on the metaphorical journey you have just taken. This gives you time to pause after the event, to process what you've read, and to contemplate the new ideas and approaches to which you've been introduced.

You have now encountered many suggestions, stories, and practical tips on effective business communication. You've been trekking the 'Connect, Convince, Convert' trail, putting one foot in front of the other as you climbed the mountain to the top of this strategic process.

Now that you have finished the book, I encourage you to have your 'final night dinner' to review the journey and look back at what you've learnt, with the benefit of being able to see the whole trip. You will realise why it's so important to start with a strategy, just as I was able to see why we were made to have acclimatisation days during our ascent. You will understand how the practical tips and structures really do make a difference for your business communication, just as I now appreciate the practical advice I was given about keeping my head warm and drinking lots of water.

Review the ideas and concepts we've covered and think about how they might apply to your business. The workbooks are designed to guide you through this process and build the all-important strategy that is the starting point for effective communication. They'll give you a framework to assess your current communication performance and discover if you have any gaps, and they'll show you which forms of communication need to be your highest priority.

Share the strategies in this book with your team and discuss the ideas they generate. Use them as the starting point for a new approach to communicating your value.

If your 'final night dinner' review cements in your mind that you are the 'ideal audience' to whom this book is addressed, and you would like some more direct and personalised support, then please do get in touch. You can find out more in 'My Offer to You' in the next section, and you can get in touch with me at carolbenton@words2win.global or through LinkedIn.

I congratulate you on your journey, and I thank you for accompanying me on the trek. Like any journey, half the pleasure is in discussing it afterwards and sharing your experiences. So, wherever your next steps may lead you, I would love for you to share your stories with me. Do tell me how *Connect, Convince, Convert* has helped you and your technology business communicate your value more effectively to the customers you serve.

MY OFFER TO YOU

As you have trekked your way through the Connect, Convince, Convert process, you may have realised that your business or organisation needs additional support to complete the journey. If you still have gaps in your communication approach, but you don't have the time or resources to do the strategic work yourself, I have developed three offerings to help readers of this book communicate effectively with your target audience.

STRATEGIC CONTENT PROGRAMS

We start with strategic message planning, using the approach outlined in Chapter 4. We create and document your strategic message as the foundation for your communication.

The next step is an audit and a gap analysis that compares the new strategic message with your current communications.

From there, we create a content plan to address the gaps, using some or all of the ten formats of business communication outlined in Chapters 5 and 9. Depending on the needs of your business, I deliver one or more pieces of content to you every month.

The programs are completely tailored to your requirements, whether you're a micro, small/medium, or corporate business. They can run for 6 months, 12 months, or longer.

The outcome is clear, customer-focussed, and consistent communication that engages your target audience and helps you win more business.

MASTERCLASSES IN VERBAL COMMUNICATION

I provide practical, hands-on workshops to help you and/or your team master the art of verbal business communication.

These masterclasses include:
→ **Connect in One Minute:** On creating an impactful elevator pitch.
→ **Present with Panache:** Teaching you how to plan, prepare, and deliver a presentation that gets results.

These masterclasses can be run as small group workshops within an organisation, or as individual coaching programs.

The outcome is that your team members can confidently represent your business value in all settings, from networking events to formal company presentations.

TENDER RESPONSE WRITING

For many tech companies, responding to tenders is a key strategy for winning new business. If that's you, but you don't have the time and/or the skills to manage these responses successfully, don't worry—I can help.

I start with a 'win themes' workshop to map out your solution, differentiators, and benefits. I manage the creation of the response, gathering content from your subject matter experts and presenting it as a compelling argument. If it's a Government tender, I advise on how to address the many social and environmental questions that are now part of every tender requirement.

The outcome is that your sales teams aren't tied to their desks writing, you improve the quality of your responses, and you increase your win rate.

I work with clients around the world, so there are no geographical limitations to the companies that I help. Contact me at carolbenton@words2win.global or via LinkedIn, and I will help you use the power of words to win more business. I look forward to hearing from you.

ACKNOWLEDGEMENTS

It takes a village to raise a child, and I'd now say it requires the same to bring a book to the world. So many people contributed to the making of this book, and I owe all of them my thanks.

Firstly, to my parents who never gave me any reason to doubt that I could do anything I put my mind to. They have also each written a book, so my 'way with words' is, I imagine, genetic.

To my primary school French teacher, Mrs. Guttman, who first sparked the love of language and translation—thank you.

To Bryan Ward, who suggested I apply to IBM, thank you for introducing me to a career I never would have considered without you. To the managers and mentors along the way—Wayne Phillips, Andrew Brown, Colin Page, Jeff Ferdinands, Maree McClaren, Simon Chapple, and Nicola Commins—thank you for making my time in the world of tech so rewarding. A particular mention to my colleague at Toshiba, Noel Fidock, who sowed the seed of realising that I had valuable skills to offer. Thank you to Andrew Ford, who helped to nurture that seed into Words2Win, and to my business coach, Michele Carson, who has kept me on the right strategic track.

To my clients, thank you for putting your trust in me and for giving me many of the examples and stories I've shared in this book, which bring the theory to life. I can honestly say I don't have a single client that I don't love working with—you have made my job fun, and for that I am truly grateful.

To my fantastic editor Caitlin Freeman and book designer Maja Wolnik. Like many people, I didn't realise what an amazing job editors do. Caitlin has encouraged me, helped me shape my wayward ideas into a meaningful structure, and polished up my turns of phrase. Maja's beautiful design and layout has helped you, dear reader, keep turning the pages. She has enhanced my words and made this book into the beautiful publication it is.

To my beautiful children, Billy and Juliette. Thank you for letting me share your stories here, and I hope you know that everything I do is for you.

Finally, to my wonderful husband Scott. You put your career on hold to support mine, you believe in me, you encourage me, you support me, and you help me lighten up and see things in perspective. Thank you for it all.

ABOUT THE AUTHOR

Carol Benton is the founder of Words2Win. As a business communication consultant with over 30 years of industry expertise, she helps her clients to win more business by clearly articulating their value. She does this by helping them to develop a consistent message strategy, creating content for all customer-facing aspects of their organisation, and teaching them how to communicate more effectively in written and verbal formats.

Communication is at the heart of every successful business, and Carol helps companies in the technology sector to connect with their audience, convince them to engage, and convert them to loyal customers.

Her expertise is based on world-class business experience and a talent for verbal and written communication. Carol spent 30 years in corporate sales and marketing—the majority with technology powerhouse and world leading brand, IBM, along with three years as General Manager (ANZ) for Toshiba Global Commerce Solutions. Carol has written, reviewed, and delivered presentations, proposals, and business content that won IBM and Toshiba millions of dollars with clients in the UK and Australia.

As well as hands-on, customer-facing experience, corporate life gave Carol unparalleled access to the best sales, marketing, and leadership training available, including education at:

→ The London Business School
→ Macquarie Graduate School of Management
→ The Chartered Institute of Marketing (UK)

Carol has a skill for 'translation'—taking an idea and representing it in the most appropriate form for the audience. She can quickly get to the heart of what a solution offers, and then she helps her clients to translate from 'what we do' to 'what benefits the customer'.

She understands the importance of structure, clarity, and impact in written communication, and she is highly adept at distilling big ideas and plans into executive-level summaries.

She has a passion for effective communication and a drive to find the words to communicate to people in terms that mean the most to them. She used this talent in her corporate career, representing IBM in print and television media. Her love of communication started when she learned foreign languages in her youth—she discovered a passion for the ability to translate and to talk to people in their own language.

Carol's expertise is based on a passion for language, combined with 30 years in international corporate sales and industry-leading business education.

Carol is a languages graduate with impeccable attention to detail for structure, vocabulary, and grammar. She speaks fluent French and has a working knowledge of several other languages.

She is a highly capable public speaker and is qualified as a Competent Toastmaster with Toastmasters International. She speaks and coaches regularly with business networking groups in the UK and Australia.

Above all, Carol believes that language is a powerful business tool, and her passion is helping her clients find their Words to Win.

Lightning Source UK Ltd.
Milton Keynes UK
UKHW021007110522
402808UK00002B/2